Cold Hands, Warm Heart

Tess Burrows

Eye Books

Published by Eye Books Ltd 2010
7 Peacock Yard
Iliffe Street
London
SE17 3LH

Tel. +44 (0) 207 708 2942
www.eye-books.com

ISBN: 9781903070789

Design by Emily Atkins
Edited by Martha Ellen Zenfell

The events and opinions in this book originate from the author.
The publisher accepts no responsibility for their accuracy.

British Library Cataloguing in Publication Data
A catalogue record for this book is available from the British Library

Printed and bound in Great Britain by J F Print Ltd.

eyeOpener

Eye Books publishes books that record the travels of people who set out on adventures that not only test their physical and mental strengths, but more importantly change the way they look at the world. Sometimes these stories go beyond uncovering physical or spiritual reward, and instead become missions to achieve a greater good, and alter the perceptions of many along the way.

Travelling requires us all to carry something. On the road we take with us what belongings we need for the journey and our personal experiences which we use as guides to interpret every new place we encounter. Along with these things Tess Burrows takes with her an extra piece of luggage – a message of hope, peace and understanding that is amplified by the hundreds of Peace Messages she intends to deliver on her expedition.

Cold Hands, Warm Heart is more than the account of a sixty-year old woman's incredible attempt to race to the South Pole, but also the tale of that same woman carrying a collective call for compassion through elements too daunting for most of us to withstand. Tess not only tests her strength and will by exposing herself to constant physical duress and extreme temperatures, but also by adding the expectations of those who have entrusted her with delivering their Peace Messages. Yet it is within her promise to transport those messages that she finds the power to endure endless bodily strain, *Cold Hands,* and her warm internal spirit is the insulation shielding her from unbearably treacherous cold and the harsh wind chill, *Warm Heart.*

With her quest to reach the South Pole Tess demonstrates that the journey can be about more than individual gains or enlightenment. She does not travel as one person within a group but as the embodiment of all those who spur her onward in hopes of raising awareness for the Earth and creating a better life for the children of the Earth.

It is our goal in publishing stories like Tess' that Eye Books challenges the way we see things. It is our hope that our readers will open their eyes to new places and experiences that differ from what they would ordinarily find. With this book you can join in on the shared journey that is already taking place on every snow covered path and at the turn of every page.

Dan Hiscocks
Publisher Eye Books

www.eye-books.com

Dedication

*With love for my granddaughters, Elsie and Bess, and all the children of the world,
for their future on this Earth, in peace and in harmony.*

This page marker is a sketch of an ice crystal at the South Pole, illustrating harmonious six-sided configuration.

Contents

Foreword
by Sir Ranulph Fiennes O.B.E.
April 2009

Some things are timeless; like stories of adventure and endeavour which continue to stand out and stir the human heart. It particularly applies to those about people pushing out boundaries and attempting to make their seemingly impossible dreams come true.

This is one such account. It has a fairytale nature that touches us, saying – well, if a 60-year-old grandmother can set out on a quest to try and help the Earth by joining a race and walking to the South Pole, then it's possible to find the energy to walk down the road, or the guts to keep going when there is pain, or the courage to knock on a neighbour's door to offer help.

Each of us is on our own archetypal South Pole journey. We have setbacks and heartaches to cope with, blizzards and intense cold to survive, crevasses to avoid, exhaustion to overcome, relationships in times of stress to manage, higher ground to climb.

These pages offer inspiration to put in the extra mile, to keep striving, to work through the struggle and to believe in the pot of gold at the end of the rainbow. They give a taste of "life on the edge" in the Antarctic, of the beauty and stark tranquillity of this precious wilderness, and, ultimately, an invitation to enjoy the race which we are all running anyway, the race for the peace and harmony of our planet.

Map of the Antarctic

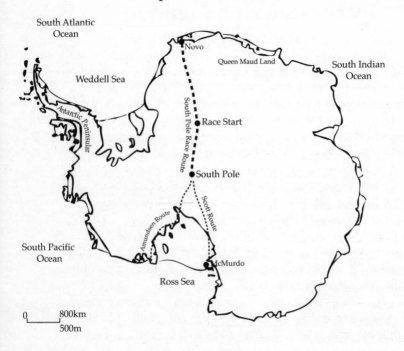

South Atlantic
Ocean

Novo

Queen Maud Land

South Indian
Ocean

Weddell Sea

Antarctic Peninsular

South Pole Race Route

Race Start

South Pole

Amundsen Route

Scott Route

South Pacific
Ocean

McMurdo

Ross Sea

0   800km
     500m

Letter of Introduction
from Tess Burrows

Dear Reader,

I send you loving greetings.
Each one of us lives on the Earth. This is our home. I passionately believe that it is possible for us all to exist here in a state of peace and harmony – not only with ourselves but also with the environment.

This is why my partner Pete and I run a small charitable organisation known as **Climb For Tibet**, supported by our chief patron His Holiness the Dalai Lama.

At a practical level we raise funds for the building of schools in Tibet. We also collect Peace Messages which both children and adults write for us in the form of prayers, wishes, hopes and pledges for the environment, in the spirit of individuals making a difference. We undertake to carry these to high places to speak them out. This is like the Tibetan tradition of flying Peace Messages on prayer flags from the highest places possible, as a way of sending blessings far and wide to reach all beings.

I believe that this, along with multitudes of other initiatives, large and small, is helping in the race for the peace and harmony of our world; that the cold hands of greed, separation and fear are being transformed by the warm heart of sharing, unity and love.

But if you felt that you wanted to try and take Peace Messages to the ends of the Earth, indeed to the South Pole, how would you *ever* go about it?

This is my story.

Tess

Antarctic Christmas

23rd December, 2008

The wind came in the night. We had gone to sleep with the sun blazing, filtering its orange glow through the side of the tent, comforting and even hot. I had stirred a few times, restless and aware of a sound, pulling my headband lower over my eyes and ears, not wanting to know. It was hard to get a sense of when it was morning in this land of continuous light, but the alarm hadn't gone off. The clock we'd bought in Cape Town didn't seem to work. Can't say I blame it. It wasn't designed for extreme cold, but for big soft beds, lazy cups of tea and books to read. We were relying on my explorer watch, though sometimes I sleep through that alarm. I felt for it on my wrist to touch its solid reality. It had been a gift to me from my tiny granddaughter holding my heart strings tight, far away on the other side of the world.

There's that weird sound again. Was it a roar? No, more like an animal howling. Oh my goodness! My eyes shot open in fright. My blood raced and pounded through the veins. I sat up and instinctively moved closer to Pete. This was scary. The tent was shaking as though an unseen force had it in its teeth. The sides were flapping loudly. I shivered as fear took hold of my body, settling in as if it owned the place. There was a ferocious slooshing of snow outside and the wind was yelling. Then I saw it.

"Pete! Wake up. The tent's caving in!"

The whole side near where he was lying was squashed in. Wind and snow together were forcing it down.

"The wind's changed. It's blowing from the east," he said, now wide awake. "It was due south on the rear of the tent last night when we made camp. That's a 90-degree shift."

"What can we do about it?" My voice trembled as I tried to control it.

"Not a lot. But we'll see how the new tent stands up to a side wind. This is a test of the design in these conditions. Don't worry; it'll be okay."

Great. We were about to freeze to death and he was interested in the design. But, as always, there was something about Pete's rock-like strength that calmed me. He was my knight-in-shining-armour, always there to protect me.

Just then, there was a muffled voice from outside. "You okay in there?" It was the Norwegian guide whom we had dubbed the Warrior (not because he'd walked to the North Pole eight times, but because of his Mohican haircut).

"Yeah, 'cept the side's caving in."

"I'll tighten the guy-lines. That'll help. Tent down as usual. We're leaving at 10am."

We were going out in this weather?!

There was nothing for it but to go through the motions of breakfast and packing up. This process would take us more than two hours. Even though we had melted snow into water to fill up all the flasks and bottles last night, we still needed at least two litres of water for the porridge and drinks now. This meant that we had to melt more snow so that we could set out with six full containers. Then the stoves, so crucial to our survival, had to be packed away carefully, so that they weren't bashed on whatever adventures the day's journey might bring. And all the gear had to be ready to be stowed in the canoe-like sledges we pulled behind us – our pulks.

I fiddled about with what I was going to wear, procrastinating as long as I could. Once outside there would be little chance to change, especially in this blizzard. Taking anything off would not only give the wind an opportunity to blow it away but increase our vulnerability to cold. Anyway, doing anything with big gloves on wasn't easy. At this stage – two days before Christmas – we were on the acclimatisation trek with the other racers, being guided through the worst of the crevasses. So it was useful to try out different combinations of kit to see what worked best as we needed to be as efficient as possible up on the plateau once the race itself started.

This was the South Pole Race. My pulse quickened even more at the thought of it. A race to the South Pole hadn't been attempted for nearly a hundred years, since Robert F. Scott and Roald Amundsen set off in 1911. Everyone knew how that had ended; Captain Scott and his companions had not returned. Nobody knew now if this race was possible. How had I *ever* become involved in something so terrifying? Pete and I were one of the six teams taking part. When the race started, we would be faced with four weeks of long days pulling pulks across 500 miles of the world's largest, coldest and emptiest ice sheets – the Antarctic.

Now we were confronting our first blizzard. Things could get a whole lot worse. Already I had fear seeping through every cell of my body. And hidden away somewhere in my mind were tales of 200 miles per hour katabatic winds, of tents ripping and blowing away, explorers falling into fathomless crevasses, unspeakable frostbite and gangrene... all bundled up into a knotted dread of the unknown. On top of that was the thought that once the race started, apart from one resupply checkpoint, Pete and I would be entirely on our own.

Trying to concentrate on the job at hand I chose my headwear – a silk balaclava and my windproof cap which had a Tibetan flag on it. I felt good in that; it always reminded me of our greater purpose. In my mind the flag was synonymous with peace. We were on a peace mission. We had collected 1,300 Peace Messages from individuals, including many children, promising to do all we could to take them to the South Pole to speak out. This is in the Tibetan spirit of flying Peace Messages on prayer flags from the highest places to send out blessings of peace and harmony to all beings. Thoughts of our mission gave me mental strength which I hoped was somehow going to see me through, along with other things, like wearing my cherry coloured neck warmer that I hadn't taken off since arriving in the Antarctic. I had bought it with part of a shop voucher that my sons and their girlfriends had given me for my 60th birthday. It represented my connection with them all, a holding of closeness.

I pulled on my salopettes over thermals and a fleece. Then went through the foot process of thin and thick socks, followed by felt liners, boots that took ages to lace and the orange and maroon gaiters that I loved. This was followed by a windproof jacket and finally, goggles with a face mask flap, so that I had no skin exposed on my face. Finally, the hood of the jacket. It was all horribly claustrophobic; I could barely breathe or see.

At this stage, going outside was inescapable. We unzipped the tent's inner and outer doors and chucked our gear into the little spot which was sheltered by its end. Today I was the last one out, so I rolled up the mats. Then it was a matter of transporting everything into the pulks. Except... where are the pulks? We definitely left them in this spot last night. Ah, I could just see the tops of the red covers poking out of the wild scene that greeted us. It may not snow much in the Antarctic, but that's not to say there isn't a lot of snow about. The wind picks up every bit it can and uses it as a battering ram against the slightest impediment in its path. Spindrift. This gradually builds up into huge piles.

The gale whacked into us as we grabbed the shovels and dug out the pulks. There would be a lot of extra snow to pull today as we hadn't closed the pulk-covers very well last night and it was too hard to tip it all out now. Never mind. I went into a frenzy of packing the gear and then working on the tent, which had to be dug out and rolled up. Heaving a sigh of relief we fixed it to the top of Pete's pulk.

From nowhere, Tony appeared. I had forgotten that the organisers and film crews would be camping discreetly nearby with the vehicles. "Well done, guys, good job." Praise indeed from Tony, the organiser of the race. He was as tough as they come, an ex-commando logistics expert who had trained soldiers in Arctic warfare and police in Iraq. "Get inside your emergency shelter until everybody's ready," he ordered.

The emergency shelter was a round nylon sheet tied to the end of my pulk. When undone it started flapping madly trying to take off. After much wrestling we tamed it so that we could sit underneath on the end of the pulk with bits of the shelter secured by our boots. It was noisy but gave us a few minutes respite from the wind. Then I noticed how hot I was. Too many clothes on; I was steaming, but there was nothing I could do about it. The consequence was my goggles misted up so I could only see from one corner of my left eye. How annoying.

We compressed the emergency shelter back into its bag, put on our skis, attached harnesses and pulks and huddled together with everybody else to hear the instructions for the day.

"This is great weather isn't it?" shouted the Warrior gleefully.

"'Tis if you're Norwegian," Ben responded loudly to James and Ed. They were in the celebrity team, QinetiQ, which was being filmed for the BBC documentary *On Thin Ice*. I could see why Ben was a TV presenter. He always had a good comment for the cameras, even in these appalling conditions.

"Stay close together and keep an eye on those near you," the Warrior said. "The still air temperature is only minus nine degrees Centigrade, but the wind speed of 35 miles per hour is bringing the wind chill down to minus 25°C. Stay covered up."

I could only just hear him above the roar of the wind, but I needed no prompting to cover up. What's it going to be like when it's seriously cold? I knew that the coldest still air temperature ever recorded had been here in the Antarctic. A mind-blowing minus 89°C. Even if we experience only half of that it's going to be nasty, especially with the wind chill.

My face was already really cold. This didn't change

throughout the day as we skied, although I found I had to work hard to hold the pace, battling the wind-driven snow coming awkwardly from the side. Soon I was sweating. I thought of the standard training advice: "You sweat, you die", and hoped that this would be an exception. I was far too busy concentrating on keeping up with everyone to contemplate death just at the moment.

Stopping skiing was a nightmare. I became chilled immediately. The first break we put up our emergency shelter, which felt good when we were inside, but it took us so long to do it that there was no time left in the 10-minute break for eating. Gaz thoughtfully helped us take it down. He, Christian and Gary, of team Danske Bank, had put theirs up too and continued to do so successfully. It looked as though it was more easily done in a team of three. The only other team of two people was Missing Link. These were the Norwegian boys, Stian and Rune. They gave the impression that they could survive even if traversing the Antarctic solo.

On the next stop we just faced away from the wind, suffered the cold and tried to get into our supplies and moving again in as short a time as possible, which became our standard method. On this occasion we had entertainment. The Warrior suddenly went flying by without his pulk, skiing as though he was running barefoot on a beach at a tremendous rate and disappeared into the oblivion of white – sky or snow it was impossible to tell. What was that all about? Had he become bored with our plodding pace? After a while he returned.

"Sorry Ed, I couldn't catch your glove. I had to give up or I'd've lost you all." It had been a vital over glove. Luckily, QinetiQ had brought a couple of spares. It was a lesson to us all. In the blink of an eye the wind can eat a crucial piece of equipment that could lead to frostbite... or worse.

I struggled on wearily through the day, battling the blizzard and not being able to see much because of misted up goggles. Even when I could there was nothing except the fuzzled outline of a pulk in front and a skier to my side. The whiteout made everything strange. Without discernable form or shadow we were in a multi-dimensional cloud, and I felt quite disorientated. It was difficult to tell what was up or down, near or far away.

Sometimes when everything seems crazy bad and it feels like the world is caving in there's one lovely thing that shines through and changes the day around. Making that thing seem almost magical.

We sat huddled for another break after a hard two hour session across very heavy snow. I pulled down my goggles to wipe them. At that precise moment right out of the swirling mists came the most beautiful bird I've ever seen. It was pure white from wing tip to wing tip. Soaring gracefully to within a metre of my face as though dropping a message, it connected a coal black eye with mine for a lingering second and was gone. It all happened so fast, I wondered if it was real.

"Did you see that, Pete?" I declared excitedly. "It was so wonderful."

"See what..."

"Did anyone see that bird?" I shouted.

All I received back was "What bird?"

It had to be a welcoming angel, surely.

After two more hours, we'd done a total of eight hours on the move, and it was time to make camp. The Warrior gathered us around. "We've had slow conditions. We really need to keep going for another couple of hours. Is everyone happy with that?"

I wondered if I dare say anything. I knew I'd had enough and had been mentally preparing to stop as planned, though everyone else seemed so strong and energetic (not to mention youthful) I thought they would probably want to keep going. But my body needed to build up day strength slowly rather than in a macho way. "It would be nice to camp here," I ventured.

"Okay, let's compromise and do one more hour. By the way, did anyone see the snow petrel? They come inland to nest in the rocks in the mountains here."

"So that's what it was, a snow petrel. How lovely. A good

sign, I think."

"Nah," he said sceptically. "Signs are inventions of the mind."

They may be inventions of the mind, but it was a sign to me, a welcome from the land.

That evening it took hours to dry out our soaked gear. We melted the water for the meals in the end porch and then brought two stoves into the inner tent and positioned them under the hanging net piled high with wet stuff. Snow seemed to have got everywhere. Even the inside of my jacket was lined with ice from the sweat. It wasn't going to be much fun if we had to sort this out every night. By the time we wriggled into our sleeping bags with the wind still grunting and whining and the snow hissing, fatigue had become stronger than anxiety. I just hoped that the blizzard lizard would have scurried away by the morning.

It hadn't.

"It's marginal, going out in these conditions," said the Warrior as we gathered for the day's instructions, kitted out and ready to go. From what I could see of his face he was enjoying this. "By the way, does anyone not feel safe?"

I thought I'd keep quiet this time.

Today was Christmas Eve. I wished for a less white Christmas.

By mid afternoon the storm had abated and the sun was shining. There was a collective sigh of relief. Everyone relaxed, took off their hoods and chatted. Now we could enjoy the freedom of visibility and gaze at a stunning white sea and distant mountains. Everyone, that is, except for Mark, who with Simon represented Ireland in team South Pole Flag. Mark is blind. After the whiteout conditions I appreciated a little more of what he was going through, even though he always seemed to be cheery and unfazed, which only increased my admiration. I thought of the time he'd told me that it had taken the full 10 years since he went blind to accept who he now was, to stop looking backwards and to get on with living life. He's only 32, but is now a top motivational speaker who helps others find their own positive paths in life. Mark has found the freedom of inner visibility. His story inspired me to look for more strength within myself.

The return of the light pleased the film crews as well. They would lie in wait for the cavalcade to pass by with cameras and sound dogs at the ready, then rush ahead to position themselves to do the same all over again. At first it felt strange, but now I accepted it as normal to be in this great wilderness of thousands of square miles devoid of any hint of humanity and have a film crew suddenly pop up in your face.

We had now reached an altitude of around 1,500 metres and barely noticed the climb. In fact, the snow today had been flat and easy going, but it doesn't do to become complacent in the Antarctic. We'd been skiing for nine hours. High cloud had blocked out the sun and everything had taken on a grey hue. The temperature had dropped considerably. My body was ready to stop, particularly as I was feeling a painful blister on my right big toe. The Warrior gathered us together and I thought for the first time he almost looked concerned.

"Watch out here. Crevasse field. Come back into single file. Ski exactly where I ski. And take care on the ice."

It was ice alright. Well ribbed blue ice, full of little crevasses, lines crossing and cracking all over the place. Skis skidded in all directions making it tricky to stay upright and taking lots of concentration. We were nearly through when I noticed that someone had taken their skis off and was managing much better without them. I wished I'd thought of that. It was Rachel, who was with Phil and Hylton in team Due South. She had a reputation of being tough, but I knew her to be sensitive and compassionate. It was comforting to know there was another female on the race.

Once across the most perilous ice, our worries continued. It was time to make camp, but we were still on ice with just a small covering of snow. No way were bamboo tent pegs going to go into that, or even skis. We needed ice screws and a hammer, which we hadn't brought.

"Tie your tent to your pulks," said the Warrior.

Right. And scrape up lots of snow to go round the valance. And pray for no wind. "Please Antarctica.... hold us safely," I whispered to the land. Like many explorers, being in this wild wilderness far from civilisation had already prompted a need in me to connect at a deeper level with my surroundings.

By the time we'd eaten and melted snow for the bottles it was midnight. I unzipped the inner tent and just enough of the outer tent to poke my head out, and was greeted by something wonderful: no wind. I gasped, feeling the air brittle and sharp in my lungs. Beyond our little camp I could see only snow, snow and more snow stretching out in wavelets of purple haze reaching to far-off peaks painted purple, too. The sky had cleared to blue, with long streaks of cloud in front of the sun low on the horizon burnishing with golden light. There was silence, and absolute peace. The magic touched me at a deep level with its utter beauty. I thought of all my family at the other end of the world. This was the time we usually go up the hill near my home, Plumtree Cottage, to welcome in Christmas. Merry Christmas, everyone.

Never was there a Christmas day like this one. Whilst Pete was asleep I hung up the decorations. They consisted of a piece of red tinsel which I strung across the tent and the one card that I had brought from my dear Mum. She'd been quite concerned about my going away, asking repeatedly why anyone would actually *want* to go to the South Pole. Her card was complete with traditional tree and snowy scene. Great, that felt more Christmassy and would be nice for Pete when he opened his eyes. Then I tore out a page from my diary and wrote him a card, wrapping it around a squashed piece of chocolate I'd been saving for the occasion. In the morning it added to our decorations along with a card that Pete had bought me in Cape Town, usefully written in Afrikaans, as well as one that team Due South had made us. We were touched by the festive gesture, but it smelled so strongly of glue I felt woozy (interesting team tactics).

Then we had a visit from Santa and his elves – Tony and the camera crew in silly hats. They were bringing each person a tiny parcel of Christmas cake and a little bottle of brandy. I took one whiff and went woozy again, so Pete thought he'd better have double rations. After all, he was meant to be convalescing after two major operations. He found a little email from his brother wrapped around the cake, which made him feel emotional and long to hear from his four children. I felt for everyone being apart from wives, girlfriends and families, particularly those who had children. Although Pete and I enjoyed the Christmas hugs with the rest of our racing family, we were glad we had each other.

The still air and sunshine brought sparkles to the snow and also to our faces. We put our sleeping bags outside. The air is so dry in Antarctica that it grabs any moisture immediately. Due to the low atmospheric pressure, sublimation occurs. This is a process whereby a solid goes directly to a gas, missing out the liquid state – useful as it means that snow goes straight to water vapour without getting everything wet. We tipped out everything we had onto the snow, as did all the teams. Any passing person would have thought there was a car boot sale on.

Pete decided that he was going to celebrate with a snow bath. Cavorting naked in the snow, he tricked his body into thinking that it was having a wash. His feet and ears knew otherwise, though, as he still had on tent bootees and earphones, listening to groovy music. Perhaps it was a good thing that there were no passersby. Must have been strong brandy.

There was a lovely sense of togetherness and purpose that Christmas Day as we all set off. I wound the tinsel around my head to mark the occasion and also cut some for Gaius, my penguin mascot sitting on the front of the pulk. He looked about as dashing as a penguin could look. It was warm enough to not wear jackets and face masks, which felt so good. Hoodless, I could turn my head from side to side and enjoy the amazing beauty that only dazzling sun on snow can bring to a landscape. It also meant that we could be sociable, chatting to others coming and going in varying assortments of coloured nose guards.

Ed had gone for seasonable red felt with a slight upturn on the cheeks. It was good to speak with him about the family gatherings that we were both missing, and as he was about the age of my sons it filled a little bit of the gap. He was lucky to be on the race, picked out of the nationwide selection process that James and Ben had put on to find their third team member, with TV cameras rolling. But now he had to cope with being thrust in the limelight. Today, he was having to wear a camera around his neck that stuck out half a metre in front of him on poles secured from his waist. Tinsel might have been more Christmassy.

How often have I had Christmas dinners and not appreciated them. I mean really, *really* appreciated them. As the day wore on and we trudged across well hidden crevasse fields and up long inclines that became more and more taxing, blisters rubbing and thigh muscles aching, the thought of Christmas dinner became more and more appealing. I remembered the year we had decided to only have a bowl of rice on Christmas Day and send money to charity instead. That was the one that stuck in my mind most of all. By not having something I was appreciating it more than when I had it. I started talking to anyone next to me about nut roasts, vegetarian sausages, roast potatoes and parsnips, steamed vegetables and lashings of gravy... they then told me to shut up. No one wanted to be reminded of what we were missing.

We skied for only eight hours, though a bit faster than yesterday and came down into a wide open bowl surrounded by stunning mountains. To the south they were iced with snow. To the west they rose like rock fortresses inviting exploration. A few wispy clouds paced the sky which shone with so much light that if I looked up I had to screw up my eyes. The snow itself was wind-flattened to glistening slabs. And the air was so clear it sparkled. This was our camp sight.

As we were putting up our tent, Tony appeared and thrust a satellite phone at me.

"Right. You're allowed one quick phone call."

"Wow. Thank you." I knew that it would be pot luck to catch any of my sons near a land phone, but wonderfully I found my youngest, Marco. On these occasions it's all too easy to talk drivel. I was being filmed as I spoke, but I still talked drivel. In the middle of a list of all the people to send love to, I reached granddaughter Elsie. And promptly burst into tears.

"Everyone's okay, Mum. We're all thinking of you and sending love... and to Pete, too. I'll be there at Heathrow to pick you up. Love you loads." And he was gone.

I hadn't realised touching in to the family at the other end of the world would mean so much to me and how often it would give me strength in the days ahead.

It wasn't until after we'd eaten our packs of sheep-poo casserole that the film director, Alexis, put his head through the tent door. He'd had a tough day missing his family, too.

"Wondered if you two would like a Christmas pudding."

Would we ever! It was the best I'd ever tasted. Alexis was now a friend for life.

It was then that I opened the Christmas cake that I'd saved and found an email message from my brother, Graham. Another little tear escaped.

The Christmas weather miracle continued into Boxing Day. We woke to little wind and it was still warm, only around minus 10°C, though the sky had clouded over. On setting off, the first task ahead was a very steep hill. To young men, a hill is an irresistible challenge to prove themselves by going at a flat-out pace. To a granny, it's an "Oh help", so I went with a steady plod. This was where my relative lack of strength really showed up. Also my bad technique. I reached the top last in the line and sweating heavily. Tony, who'd been watching everyone's style, came and tried to help me.

"Thrust from the hips," he advised, "and be more upright, so you won't get neck strain." I didn't like to tell him that I'd tried all the correct ways of moving on skis but my body just wouldn't do it.

We were now on a wide plateau and going up more gently. The temperature was beginning to drop, and it was actually snowing fresh snow, but the wind was holding off. I concentrated on trying to keep moving and keep up. As I was close to the Warrior, I asked him about my technique.

"Relax and believe in what your body wants to do. Think of something else and your body will work out the right way for you personally."

Thank goodness. My kind of language. I could relate to that technique. Around 3pm I went through some sort of barrier and felt great, as though I could keep going at a strong pace forever. The gradual build up had worked for me, even though for many of the others it had been frustratingly slow.

That night, we checked out the day's distance. In 10 hours we had covered 18 miles. This was more than the minimum mileage that we needed to do every day during the race. We were confident about the distance. All things looked possible.

But I had forgotten...

Sometimes the universe has other plans.

Unfinished
Business

16th April, 2006

My quest to reach the South Pole had actually begun two and a half years earlier at the other end of the Earth.

I knew, even then, that it was the most disappointing moment of my life.

The racers were jostling to stand in line. Behind them were pulks bulging with all the equipment that would be needed to ski the 368 miles to the magnetic North Pole. I shivered, not from the minus 25°C temperature, but from the ice knots in the pit of my stomach that were giving a chill from within.

I stood silently, Pete by my side. I could hear the teams speaking amongst themselves, the laughter and the banter. They were about to ski over the line of rope that had been placed as a marker between two sponsor flags flapping merrily in the wind. The race was about to start.

That's where we should have been.

The charge began. Everyone rushed off, swinging ski-sticks and marching legs, swept up in the excitement, cheering, arms punching the air. One person did a cartwheel expressing the exuberance and joy of the moment (unless he just slipped).I stared, mesmerised in disbelief. My mind was almost floating out of the back of my head as though it couldn't bear to stay in this place of despair. We had been preparing for this moment for two years; two years of building up fitness, of struggling to find sponsors, of scrimping and saving, of charity fundraising, of choosing and testing the gear, and most of all, two years of collecting Peace Messages. I had thought of little else over all this time.

The racers became smaller as they pulled away, dark figures settling down to a steady pace, stark against the great expanse of white. They crossed the flat sea ice and headed towards the hills, which sloped invitingly off to the north. Angrily I wiped away a tear, my eyes never leaving the scene until it was one of small black dots disappearing over the distant horizon. My world shattered into a thousand pieces, brittle and cold, like the ice at my feet.

Pete turned and put his arms around me, breaking the silence.

"I'm so sorry, Tess," he said. I clung to him then and sobbed uncontrollably.

We had been pulled out of the North Pole Race for medical reasons. Pete had experienced what he called a palpitation. The medical term is *Supraventricular tachycardia*. This is a sudden quickening of the heart rate, which continues for an indeterminate period of time and then just as suddenly stops, leaving the body to carry on as fit and as strong as ever. He had experienced it on and off for a few years and had learnt to live with it even during mountain adventures and in far-off places. Whilst it was happening, his body worked at less than full capacity and he felt light-headed, so he would either keep going gently or sit for a while – sometimes minutes, sometimes hours – until it righted itself. I accepted it too, as just one of those things.

Pete had been careful to follow the right procedures. He had been signed off by his home doctor as fit and well to go to the North Pole and informed the race doctor, Deirdre, about it before all the training on the ice had started.

Unfortunately, a palpitation had come in the middle of the acclimatisation trek and it was something out of the ordinary that the support team hadn't experienced before. This had started a bureaucratic rigmarole between medical advisers and insurers back in England that couldn't be resolved from the Arctic.

The general upshot had been, "Pete can come to the end of the acclimatisation leg when there will be support around, but a palpitation might occur again in a gale force wind, in whiteout conditions whilst he's falling into the sea ice and Tess is being eaten by a polar bear. There is no way that he can cross that start-line and take part in the race."

That had left me without a team-mate, and it had been too late to join up with anyone else.

It was not to be.

"You've got to let go," the kind Canadian guide Matty said when we were back in the outpost of Resolute. "You've got to move on, difficult as it is. It's worse because you had so much determination to make it happen. You were all wound up holding onto your goal so tightly and for so long. That makes it harder."

Pete nodded in agreement. He had experienced the pain of disappointment on numerous occasions, mostly tempered by his own down-to-earth wisdom of knowing when to turn back on a mountain, when safety overrides the dream. He had learnt the hard way about letting go. When we had been waiting for the palpitation to stop he had suspected the implications. I remembered the way he had looked at me then, with hurt in his eyes, desperate not to let me down, desperate not to let himself down. Somehow, he had already moved on. "You just do it" was his way of tackling these situations, and he put his hand on mine, trying to give that strength to me.

I sighed heavily, blinking to stop the waiting tears. "Try screaming at the top of your voice," Matty said. "It really helps."

I looked around, furtively, at the groups of explorers, scientists and hunters at the other tables where we were all enjoying a quiet coffee in relative civilisation after long and exhausting journeys across the Arctic ice. Could be interesting, screaming here...

She continued, "You know, the main problem with visiting the Arctic is that it makes you want to go to the Antarctic."

Pete leaned forward, his interest immediately caught. "Radical! What would that cost, to go to the South Pole?"

"It's a lot more than to the North, obviously," Matty answered in a matter-of-fact way. "But if you've got a group it's not too bad. Last year we skied in with the kids and kited back." She made it sound as though it was a trip to the local supermarket. "You have to do these things with style, you know, keeping a positive spirit of adventure."

I helped myself to a couple of biscuits and chewed this thought over.

South Pole – hmmm. The words immediately conjured up feelings of cold, terrifying cold and isolation. Boldness in pitting yourself against the elements and the unknown, to explore and further the knowledge of mankind. They spoke of hardship and deprivation, of toughness and strength of character. Inexplicably, they had always stirred the adrenalin in my heart.

I remembered as a student in 1969 hearing about the first females to be at the South Pole. It had been five American scientists and a journalist. They had been flown in, so to my mind it didn't really count, but I remembered the twinge of "Oh, I'd like to be there." It had touched a longing, a desire to tread on unexplored land and feel the challenge of an impossible dream.

Impossible – until now.

Now, we had some experience and training in the harsh polar environment and, with someone like Matty to guide us, I could visualize a South Pole journey that could manifest a dream into a reality. And it could further our work with the Peace Messages. Okay, finance would be a huge hurdle, but there were means of raising it, like sponsorship.

A tiny spark of excitement ignited at the possibility, licking at the edges of the black cloud of disappointment. Maybe, just maybe, the South Pole could be a way out of this failure at the North Pole.

Heart Song

It took several weeks to recover both physically and mentally from the Arctic trip. Thoughts of never-ever-again need time to disperse, leaving just the good memories. This was no exception. Time worked its magic. However, there was one concern that stayed with me – the warming of the Arctic environment. We had witnessed the unseasonal melting of the ice and continued to hear about it from friends there. We'd had temperatures considerably higher than expected. The summer period without sea ice was two weeks longer than normal. This meant fewer seals. So polar bears went hungry and seemed to be on their way to being wiped off the face of the Earth.

Our Peace Messages are all about harmony, both for humanity and the environment. So many of our Arctic Messages were pledges for the environment that had been written by children, some including beautifully coloured pictures. These were promises to make a difference in their lives, such as "I will walk to school to save petrol and help the Earth." Others were on the theme of "Love to polar bears." These Messages touched my heart. I knew I couldn't just stop the work of trying to raise awareness and make a difference to the Earth; we had to continue. Perhaps we could find a new high spot from which to send out the next lot (somewhere warm would be nice).

This is how we raise the money for Climb For Tibet. People

give us sponsorship and their personal Messages to take on our next peace climb. Over the last few years we had raised enough funds to build six schools in Tibet. Our patron, the Dalai Lama, says that the education of young children in Tibet is a good way of trying to help the structure of this stricken country. Ever since communist China had taken over Tibet in 1949, Tibetans have been second-class citizens in their own land and struggled to hang onto their culture, their religion and, indeed, their very essence. By providing schooling for youngsters with no chance of learning to read or write, we felt that at least we were contributing to a way forward and hope for a future.

In the meantime, in our privileged western lives we had nice ordinary things to organise, like Pete's 60th birthday party. It was a merry get together of family and friends, all those who had recently supported us with sponsorship and were interested in how we had got on.

"Yeah, we had a great time in the Arctic."

It didn't help that everyone then asked, "So, where are you going next?"

Why couldn't people ask "What are you having for dinner tonight?" or "How are your bunions?" or "Does your cat have fleas?" Why was it always "Where are you going next?" This demanded an answer so I found myself joking, "Well, we've done north, so I guess it'll have to be the South Pole."

South Pole. There we are again.

Hmmm, I wonder what it would be like to really push myself in those conditions. What new mental terrain would I discover? After all, I'd just been denied the possibility of exploring that in the Arctic.

Something in my head shouted, "Don't be crazy. That's not logical. To go to the South Pole you need to be wealthy, you need to be young, you need to be strong and you need to be fit. You're not any of those things. That's not much of a start, is it? Anyway, Pete's unlikely to be able to do anything as extreme again and you wouldn't want to go without him."

"Well," my heart replied, "if there's something that you really, really want to do and it feels right, then you should do it."

I let the internal discussion simmer over the next few weeks.

Then we heard news that Tony, who had been the operations director of the North Pole Race, was planning to organise a race to the South Pole. Matty was to be involved, too. If one really, really wanted to go to the South Pole and had nothing better to do, then this would seem a good way to do it.

Well, I thought, to carry out a peace climb is a powerful reason for heading to the southern end of the Earth, except for the ticklish question of whether the South Pole is a particularly high place. In fact, it is nearly 3,000 metres above sea level, due to the laying down of huge amounts of snow. I tried picturing the world upside down to give a better sense of climbing up. It looked strange but okay. Hang on, which way is up, anyway? It's only been convention that north is at the top since the second century when the Greek mapmaker Claudius Ptolemy decided to put north at the top. Which way up were we spinning through space before that? On Alien maps the South Pole may well be at the top.

More important to my thinking were the plane journeys, which would drastically mess up my personal carbon footprint. Though maybe I was still in credit from the six million trees that my husband Lawley and I had been responsible for planting in Australia during my time there as a forester. I tried to rationalise with some positives. I can usually rely on mental strength, I surmised, and most importantly I know that I would feel supported spiritually.

"Is that it? Is that all you can come up with?" the sceptical voice inside my head shouted. "This is the South Pole, for goodness sake. People die there. It's the coldest place on Earth! You know you have bad circulation and get cold just sitting at your computer for a couple of hours – your fingers don't work properly and your body seizes up. In the Antarctic, you wouldn't be able to rely on anybody else. You would have to be able to do all the technical things that you're completely hopeless at. This is serious stuff. You're one of those women who stand beside their car looking pathetic when they have a puncture, hoping for some strong man to happen by. You cannot afford to be pathetic, otherwise you would be putting people's lives at risk. Most of all, you need great physical strength which you will never have."

I sighed. Something in me really did want to do it.

One night I had a dream:

I am running in a race looking for my sports drink. How can I run a race without Empact?

I am running up and down huge switchbacks. I feel fearful. Gradually, I develop a way to cope by taking long strides in the air which leads to flying. Wow, what a difference that makes. I do somersaults in the air just for the joy of it.

People are staring at me in awe and wonder. "Look," I say, "it's dead easy. There's no problem if you don't take on fear. All you have to do is relax and believe you can do it."

It had been a long time since I had remembered a dream so vividly. The message was clear. All I had to do was relax and believe. Somehow I missed the bit about fear.

The next day I was chatting to my lovely neighbour, Mary, over the wooden garden fence. Everyone should have a Mary as a neighbour, with a giving nature like hers to aspire to. Even though she struggles with multiple sclerosis, the debilitating disease that numbs nerve endings, she is always cheery and offering help. This was particularly welcome as she has a technical mind which is good at advising my untechnical one.

"What're you up to?" I asked, enjoying the feeling of warm sunshine on my bare arms and feet. How I loved warmth.

"I'm trying to decide what to have for lunch," she replied. "What're you up to?"

"I'm trying to decide whether to go to the South Pole," I responded.

She knew that I like doing strange things and did not come back with the question "Why?". However, in the ensuing moment of silence, I realised, there, I'd said it seriously. The South Pole was a contender and by repeating it out loud, it was more likely to happen.

The yearning didn't go away.

As long as I could remember, I'd enjoyed reading books about the polar regions. There's something about the extreme cold and the mystery. Maybe it's because it's outside the civilisation that I live in, with all its should-do rules, its complications and the physical stuff that modern man seems to find necessary. I love wild places. Though I am happy to accept, in a lazy sort of way, all the wonderful conveniences that our western society produces. My trip to the Arctic had been a taste of cold wilderness. Now it seemed I was hungry for more.

Rather than anything logical, a deep-seated part of me appeared to say "A peace climb to the South Pole makes you feel excited at an inner level. It's what makes your heart sing. This is the way to communicate with the natural systems. It's your way to help the Earth. These are the things that matter to you."

I thought of the time back in 1990 when I had undertaken a climb of the Old Man of Hoy – Britain's tallest sea stack – and hung a huge banner stating "Save the Antarctic" from this iconic spot. The climb had achieved success. Along with other groups it had helped create awareness. Conservation had triumphed over exploitation. The Antarctic Treaty Nations declared a 50-year moratorium on mining in the Antarctic.

Antarctica had called to me then.

How could I not respond now?

Commitment

We sat up in bed with an early morning cup of tea. Snug and comfortable. The sun shone in brightly through my bedroom window, catching the glass six-pointed star that swung gently, throwing rainbows across the walls. A chorus of birds sang in the new day. With my short-sighted vision I hazily followed the darting movement of little blue-tits amongst the green of the willow leaves growing rampant outside.

I was relaxed and happy. This was a favourite place, a favourite time and most of all, Pete was visiting for a few days. Although he lived 140 miles away in Suffolk we always spent a lot of time with each other, successfully living separate lives together. We had our own space and yet supported each other.

"So," he began, putting on his chairman-of-the-board voice, which rather lost its impact due to the meeting being held in pyjamas, "you've made up your mind." It was a statement of fact. He liked things in black and white. Usually he was the one who made decisions quickly whilst I would take ages waffling about in a state of uncertainty. It was as though he knew me better than I knew myself.

"Yeah, it feels right," I replied.

Without my contact lenses I could see so little that I sensed rather than watched his face for any signs of doubt or worry. It remained as usual, calm but ready to take on the world, rugged but with those boyish curls, the face of my loving soul partner.

"Where are you going to find the money?"

"No idea."

"You'll have to train far harder than you've ever trained before."

"Sure."

"And what if I don't go? What then? Will you still go?"

There was a moment's pause. "Yes, I'll still go." And a heavy, drawn-out silence.

"Well, in that case, I shall have to come to look after you."

I flung my arms around him, spilling tea all over the sheets. "That's the nicest thing anyone's ever said to me," I beamed. In spite of our decade-long relationship I was still surprised at his huge warmth of heart. He is always so positive about everything and never happier than when there's action going on. But this was more. This was a real giving of self.

Were we sane? Probably not. But the commitment was made.

When Tony put on a meeting at Newbury Racecourse to launch the South Pole Race we were there. Afterwards, we filled in the entry forms and sent off the deposit.

We were in.

There was just a certain problem. We had to find £42,300 each. This was such a huge amount of money that it seemed to have no connection to reality. I just laughed. But we started to look for corporate sponsorship immediately, writing down our team objectives:

1) To help the Earth by collecting Peace Messages and express them at the South Pole.

2) To raise charity funds: firstly for Climb For Tibet to continue building schools for underprivileged children in Tibet; secondly for the World Wildlife Fund for climate

change (after all, it had been co-founded by Captain Scott's son Sir Peter Scott); thirdly for the Multiple Sclerosis Society for compassionate relief.

Neither of us thought about actually trying to win the race.

I knew I had to be clear in my own intentions, too. So I tried to raise my personal vibration, my inner energy, by detoxifying and purifying both my body and the environment around me. Also, I meditated. I lit a few candles in my sitting room and knelt on the meditation stool that my son Paul had made for me with the encouragement "Attune to that inner stillness, Mum."

I felt that I needed clarity about my life path. In particular, I wanted to know how our South Pole journey fitted into that. So I tried to be open to loving guidance. A response came rather quickly, but not quite in the way I expected. I felt drawn into my kitchen to study the globe on the sideboard. It sat happily amongst photos of the children, old books about Tibet, pictures of mountains climbed and holding hands with the Dalai Lama, special leaves, shells, rocks and a tiny wooden penguin... all part of the clutter of loved things that make up my home. I looked at the places in the world where we had undertaken our peace climbs over the last few years:

The point furthest from the centre of the Earth – Mt Chimborazo in Ecuador

The place nearest the sun at the turn of the Millennium – Mt Aucanquilcha in Chile/Bolivia

Sacred Tibetan mountains – Kailash, Shishapangma and Everest in the Himalayas

The tallest mountain – Mauna Kea, the Hawai'i islands in the Pacific

And our journey to the top of the world in the Arctic

I turned the globe, and the soft brown colours blended gently. I held my hands around it a couple of inches out. I felt a warm tingling in my palms, the same sort of sensation that I experience when I am offering myself as a healer at the wisdom school that I work with, the White Eagle Lodge. It was as though I was sensing the energy of the peace climbs. I felt acutely aware that our two Andean peace climbs were exactly balanced out by those in the Himalayas on the opposite side of the world. And then I moved my hands to the North and South Poles. Yes, it would be perfectly balanced too when the South Pole was done. And then the third balance was the Pacific climb, which would need a climb in Africa at the equator. That would be the last piece of the jigsaw.

So, the network of light that we had helped create by taking Peace Messages to these zones of the Earth was to make a multi-dimensional six-pointed star. How lovely. It was started in 1998, South Pole would be in 2009 and Africa would fall into place after that. We would then have the whole world covered by a star of peace. It was a shining way to send love to the Earth.

I was experiencing cold sensations up and down my back that I call whooshes. I always interpret them as confirmation of things from a higher part of myself. I phoned Pete. He was busy trying to sort out the palpitation problem, making an appointment with the cardiologist.

"I've just had the most wildly exciting discovery!" I almost shouted. I couldn't sit still. I was getting more whooshes. "The Climb For Tibet network of light is shaped like a star. It's balanced across the globe. South Pole journey is confirmed. We have to be there."

For once, Pete was stunned into silence (unless he was munching a Mars bar.)

That night, our team name came to me. It was flying about in a high left corner of my mind when I caught it. The name was Southern Lights. It seemed to represent the carrying of Peace Messages like little lights for the Earth.

I had a feeling that I was being directed along a certain path and all I had to do was trust and flow with it. Advice seemed to be pouring into my mind from somewhere as though there was a door ajar and strains of music were wafting in. Hold this clarity. Maintain a higher vibration so you need less sleep (sounded useful). Hold vitality with exercise. Keep light with not overeating sluggish foods, nor watching negative TV. Focus on what you do want to happen... Okay, okay, stop! Enough advice. But I knew it was preparation. I had to really build up this body as it had never been built up before *if* I wanted to take on this mission. And yes I did want to do this mission. We had to complete the network of light. It's imperative that we do the South Pole before we get too old.

Please, may we not be too old already.

And then I saw. The universe never wastes energy. The greater picture is always perfect. Our Arctic journey had not been a failure. If we had skied to the magnetic North Pole as we had hoped, then the chances are that at our age we would have been completely exhausted. Consequently, it would have taken too much out of us to even consider tackling the South Pole. I knew then that the only way I was going to achieve this one was if I really wanted to with every ounce of my being. Tony had said at the meeting that it would work if we committed heart and soul.

Okay. Heart and soul.

New Life

The autumn leaves turned to gold and russet brown, and a chill wind came and blew them into the natural cycle of the seasons, though gently, as is the English way. Winter rested. The trees were bare, but as always never without the promise of new life with spring just around the corner.

The phone rang. It was my son, Scottie.

Scottie had been named after Captain Scott, whose nobleness of spirit he does seem to have inherited. He was meant to be a girl. Whilst I was pregnant there was no easy access to modern scanning methods in the Australian bush. So a friend had suggested an old gypsy technique of determining the sex of my baby. She held my ring on a piece of string above my tummy, watching which way round it swung. A small early girl was predicted, so when a large late boy arrived, we had no name for him. As a two-hour old baby, he had an air of a keen adventurer on the journey of life, so when Lawley said, "And how is our young Scott of the Antarctic?" Scottie was the name that stuck. He now lived with beautiful Nella in Devon near the surfing beaches, with horse, dog and cat.

"We're going to expand our tribe, Mum."

What was it to be this time? A parrot, a goldfish – hopefully not a snake.

"We're going to have a baby."

Wow!

Cold Hands, Warm Heart

I was quite unprepared for the effect that this would have on me at an emotional level. I was to be a grandmother. I felt a strong bond already, even before my granddaughter was born. It was as though I would lay down my life for her.

Was this the way that the Earth made sure that our species would survive? Was this feeling of devotion and protectiveness an evolutionary advantage? I had understood it naturally at the level of motherhood. Now I was surprised at the beauty of this connection one further generation away. Could something this precious and simple be the motivation to make the best decisions for the future of our children and grandchildren and help save the Earth?

And now I was to be the first granny to race to the South Pole. Out with the knitting.

Impossible

The "First Granny" proposal for prospective sponsors helped us through the weeks of approaching several different companies. Finally, one was keen. It was good to have the interest of a large organisation. We could offer them all sorts of benefits such as worldwide media coverage and great publicity. I was asked to come in for a meeting. Pete, who had been on the same quest in Suffolk, his neck of the woods, was excited that we were finally getting somewhere.

"So what are you going to wear to the meeting?"

"Wear? Don't know."

"You have to look business-like. You can't be your usual hippy self." He had been in the insurance industry all his life before he retired, and knew about these things.

"What do you suggest?"

"Well, I like my women in high-heeled boots and tight skirts. It always helps a meeting along."

"You've got to be joking. I'm not going like that." I was not very good at high-heels. If we went out to an evening event and I consented to wearing heels, Pete always had to carry me from the car to the building, where I would deposit them under the table at the earliest opportunity.

I submitted to buying some high-heeled sandals and we compromised on an ancient but smart pair of trousers that I found in my wardrobe. Then there was an equally ancient shirt and jacket from the days of the 60s.

"You'll have to iron the shirt."

"What!"

"You've got to make the right impression."

"We're going to the South Pole, not Claridges," I retorted, but began to search the house. I knew that there had been an iron that one of the children had used years ago.

Once dressed, I felt uncomfortable. Help, did I look normal enough? I certainly didn't feel normal. Would anyone notice? Did I have any hippy bits sticking out? Well, there was my wrist-band, a black-and-white one that I'd worn for many years to support freedom in Tibet. No way was I going to take that off.

I drove to the meeting, full of apprehension. The drive led up to a huge corporate building, where smart people in suits and the correct shoes were rushing around looking efficient. The equally smart gate-attendant in a good-looking hat directed me to the car park. I drove and drove and found a space that must have been 200 metres from the main entrance. How could I possibly walk that distance in my high-heels and look normal? I scoured the CCTV cameras, wondering if they had blank areas that I could duck through unseen. Doubtful.

I thought that carrying the shoes might look too suspicious and they wouldn't fit in my normal briefcase, but rummaging around in the car I managed to find something to put them in. "Well, I've just got to go for it," I told myself. So carrying in a tool bag what was obviously a useful exhibit for the meeting – chin up and shoulders back – I adopted an air of organised efficiency and padded across the car park to the impressive glass entrance door in my bare feet.

They liked me!

"Don't go to anyone else without telling us," they requested. After that day the exchanges continued. We were hopeful. Eventually it only had to be approved by the board.

Then came the letter.

> "We're so sorry but our budget's been cut. We're unable to sponsor you after all. We wish you the very best of luck."

Part of me was relieved. I knew that I hadn't really wanted

it enough. I didn't want to be in someone's pocket, doing it for commercial gain. I just wanted to do it for the Earth. After that, my heart went out of getting sponsorship, and the economy took a downturn for the worst anyway.

Somehow we would raise the money. Somehow...

We trickled our entire savings into the on-going payments. I felt like I was giving away my own life security, but something was telling me there was a lot more than my personal future at stake here. Anyway, we were on a financial roller coaster that we didn't dare fall off; we were committed. We had signed the competitor agreement with the South Pole Race. This was symbolised by a high-wire training day that the organisation put on. We were asked to jump off the top of a telegraph pole onto a swinging trapeze. It was a leap of faith. Yes, relax and believe. And breathe deeply.

In the meantime I brought in some income by doing talks and selling copies of my first book. This involved long hours on my feet which was useful training (I thought so anyway).

Pete worked giving climbing instruction at the Mid-Suffolk Leisure Centre and by doing some landscape gardening. His lifestyle demanded good health, which thankfully was apparent. He had seen the specialist cardiologist who had studied his heart scan and ECG report, then declared, "It's all clear and you'll live forever." The advice had been to simply accept the palpitation problem in the way that he had done for the last 12 years. It was not life threatening. Pete phoned the insurers who agreed to cover him for the race, no restrictions included. Tony told him, "We don't have an issue with it, so we don't have a problem." This was good news all round. The only proviso was "as long as the palpitations don't reoccur too much." Oh help, I worried, would they reoccur?

I knew nothing was going to slow Pete down. His energy

is always twice as much as that of someone half his age. So I wasn't surprised when the moment came that I'd been dreading.

"We have to plan the fitness training programme properly," he declared with pen in hand and a big smile. He so loved planning and putting dates for adventures in his diary. I knew that once written down there was no going back. He always made things happen.

"But it's still months and months away," I resisted. "More than a year."

"Do you want to do this or not?"

"Okay, okay." I knew that, yes, my old body would definitely take a long time to build up fitness and that it would be continuous hard work to maintain it. I longed for a 20-year-old body that could manage this so easily.

"Well, I suggest we do the Sri Chimnoy 24-hour race. Let's go for that to kick-start things."

"Running for 24 hours continuously around a track?" I groaned. "Why d'you have to choose something so impossible?" It was alright for him. He was a superhero, the right shape, tall and lean. And he'd been running long distances all his life. My running amounted to very little.

It could be great endurance training for the mind, but would my body stand up to it?

The answer was "no". I managed to run gently for the first eight hours or so, then twisted an ankle so limped and hobbled the rest of it. By the end of the 24 hours I had achieved the honour of being bottom of the leader board and only managed to cover 57 miles. Pete, in spite of a hip injury, had done 75 miles; the winner an incredible 147 miles. I was just pleased to have stayed vertical.

Sri Chinmoy said that running was a way to challenge perceived limitations and to clear the mind. My mind was so clear that I slept for three days afterwards. It was three months before my body recovered.

Meanwhile, there were other things to worry about. The South Pole Race rules stated that teams had to be three people each. This was principally a safety issue, but also one of spreading the weight of the equipment. We had a long list of people who were interested in joining us, but no one could commit financially.

This was of great concern; we wanted to be preparing and training with our final team mate. We put ourselves about on websites and in magazines and did a Christmas mail-out. We had to reach out to people to let it be known and also to raise charity funds and to collect Peace Messages. So I hired a penguin suit and waddled about undercover at the local Christmas fair. It's amazing how many people find it easier to approach a penguin rather than a person. Should we be learning something from penguins?

Donations and Peace Messages were pouring in, as well as cards with encouraging words such as:

"You are invaluable to the world. You make the rest of us think we are sane."

But still no one who could come with us. Somehow we would find a third team member. Somehow...

Our uncertainties increased when we learnt that the South Pole Race route had drastically changed from the original plan. Now we were to fly to a Russian base, Novolazarevskaya (which no one could pronounce) at 11° east. The 100-mile acclimatisation leg would start from there, after which there would be a pick-up by a smaller plane to take everyone to the start of the race, consisting of two legs of 250 miles. This meant that not only would we, crucially, now have to cover more distance on skis in the same amount of time, but that we no longer would be walking all the way from the edge of the continent. This prompted some of the contestants to drop out. More important to me was the news that Matty was no longer involved.

We didn't like it, but could do nothing about it. I often find myself fighting against changes and things that aren't how I expect them to be. Now I had to tell myself to try and flow with them. It was back to "relax and believe" that everything coming at me was drawn for my greater good. I couldn't do anything about the changes. All I could do was try to change how I saw them, change my attitude. It wasn't easy.

The 2008 New Year arrived. We sat huddled together on a little piece of carpet at the top of the hill by Plumtree Cottage, candlelight shining in the window. I gazed at the stars. My resolution was to give my utmost to achieve taking the Peace Messages to the South Pole, even though it all looked so impossible. The night sky was lit on three sides by the man-made magic of fireworks exploding, which encouraged me to keep my hopes high.

Pete's thoughts, as always, were with the feet-on-the-ground practicalities, "We have to be seriously fit. We've got a huge amount of work to do. Fitness is safety and it's also speed. I don't want to be hanging around getting cold because you're so slow." I was happier with my thoughts in the stars, but his continual reminders were beginning to get through to me. I was ready to start training again.

When he suggested kick-starting this time with a downhill skiing in the French Alps, I was all for it. Great, that's my type of training, the best way I know of to get fit.

We were joined on the trip by my brother, Graham. Life always feels good when I'm with my big brother. As a child, I only wanted to do the things that he was doing, our sisters being much younger. Throughout our lives we have shared the love of doing exciting things, though each in our own different way, and exploring why things work the way they do. He is an anchor in my world, a family tie that makes sense of everything.

He had no idea what was in store for him, until he found himself fascinated by our crevasse rescue ideas and ended up being the body on which we could practice techniques. It wasn't so bad in our hotel bedroom with the ropes attached to the door handles and the pulley system to the beds, but when he found himself hanging by a rope down an icy ravine on a heavily snowing day, his real metal was tested. Even with a triple pulley system I found it impossible to haul up his body weight. When both Pete and I finally yanked him up he was really cold, and looked more like a snowman than a brother. But his smile was warm as he croaked, "I thought you said we were going to the pub."

The skiing week was a successful fitness raising time. It was only when I had a spectacular crash and ended up with a broken rib that I had to remember to carry on regardless and never mind the pain. It was particularly frustrating as we had the important South Pole Race cold-weather training coming up in Norway.

No Way Norway

Racers and prospective racers to the South Pole were flown to Oslo at the end of January, 2008, to catch the severest weather possible. We were to be shown the Norwegian way of doing things. Following the road north for three hours into the mountains, we were dumped straight from a warm bus into a frozen world of deep snow and spruce trees thudding their loads around. It was harshly cold. Here began the first lesson: how to hang onto a sledge driven by a team of five husky-type dogs. I wasn't too sure about the controls but before there was time to worry about it, loud yelping and howling from my team heralded that we were off.

Starting on a downhill slope, I found myself immediately going at breakneck speed and hanging on for dear life to a bar attached to a sort of bucket contraption, my feet balanced precariously on two runners that were sticking out, one of which apparently held the brake. Even with my foot on it all the time it didn't seem to make any difference. Full speed ahead. There was also a second brake, a square bit of metal that needed to be chucked out like the anchor on a ship, but I had no idea how I was going to reach down for it. I needed both hands to cling tight, concentrate hard, sway right over at the corners. Help, swung too far.

Suddenly I was biting snow and my face along with the rest of my body and the sledge on its side was being wooshed along in an avalanche sort of a way. "Do not let go, whatever," had been the instructions. Well, that bit worked. My team of hot dogs stopped and looked round at me, long steamy tongues hanging out, exasperated. Who was this joke they were dragging? I righted the sledge and managed to jump on just in time as we set off again at full speed. The extra weight of snow in the sledge didn't seem to make any difference. Bend the knees, keep centre of gravity low, hang on, trees whiz by, hang on, narrowly missed that one, the next tree even closer on the bend, then "thwump" and I was on my side again. Only this time I couldn't hang on. Another team went flying by with Pete clinging on behind, hat gone, curly hair and scarf streaming out behind shouting, "Can't stop!"

"Why," I wondered when I had recovered and was sitting enjoying the warmth of Norwegian hospitality at a lovely dinner. Why was it important to experience being dragged through the snow using my head as a snow-plough? Presumably it was to give us an idea of how the Norwegian, Captain Amundsen, made it to the Pole so fast using supercharged dogs.

The manager of the Fefor Hotel welcomed us.

"I am particularly delighted to host this reception for the South Pole Race contestants, for this is where the Englishman Captain Scott trained in preparation for his 1911 expedition to the South Pole. He had trouble running his dogs."

Really?

"He had not known then that it was to be a race," continued the manager. "It wasn't until the American Admiral Peary became the first to reach the North Pole in 1909 that Amundsen, unable to now take this prize, planned to try for the South. He informed no one, not even the crew of his ship, the *Fram*, until they were mid-Atlantic in 1910.

It was only as Scott was on his way south with his ship the *Terra Nova* that he received a cablegram from Amundsen stating:

> 'Beg leave inform you proceeding Antarctic,
> Amundsen.'

The race was on. This neither prompted Scott to change

his priorities, which included an extensive programme of scientific research, nor his plans. The advancement of knowledge was very important to him, but with the great problem that he had in raising the finance, the goal of the Pole brought in more funds."

We were then introduced to the Warrior (sometimes known as Inge), who was to be the instructor for the week in Norway and for the Antarctic. Standing in the middle of the floor facing us he didn't appear to be very old, maybe mid-thirties, but his build was sturdy, his features handsome and he had an air of innate wisdom. He looked like he knew where he was going in life.

"I'm sure that this South Pole journey will be one that you'll treasure for the rest of your lives."

That sounded positive, I mean the fact that we would have some life left afterwards.

"Amundsen's way of doing things will be our way, except of course in the use of dogs which are not allowed in the Antarctic any more due to their possible effect on the seaboard wildlife."

What a pity!

"Great thanks go to our Norwegian sponsors who have supplied most of our gear. I am in the process of personally redesigning tents and shell suits. We will have the best in the world."

So was the Norwegian way to be better than the English? Time would tell. Certainly Amundsen had made it to the Pole quicker and more efficiently than Scott and more importantly had survived. Still today much debate and controversy surrounds these two courageous heroes and the decisions they made. With Norwegian and English teams on our race there was bound to be a certain amount of competition. However, I figured if a Norwegian team didn't win this race then something would be wrong, born as they were to these near-polar conditions, but then anything can happen. Remember the tortoise and the hare...

We were moved to a military training base for lectures and issued with mountains of cold-weather gear. I looked at it all piled up in boxes and laughed. It was so huge, it was hard to imagine it fitting into a pulk. This lot would even challenge the Norwegian dogs – well maybe not.

The time came to try everything out. Although I'd used wider walking skis in the Arctic, I'd never tried proper cross-country skis. I found them to be so thin and light that in the floppy Alfa boots, the same we were told as Amundsen had used, I was unstable and tottered about in a pathetic way feeling hopeless as I watched all the Norwegians jumping and doing beautiful telemark turns, relaxed and elegant in a perfect display of skill. Perhaps there would be a chance to prove myself later.

As we set out for a three-day expedition I tried to better my skiing technique. I'd been told "Concentrate on keeping the base of the skis on the snow and to slide and glide. It's important to get the motion efficient. You'll be doing over a million ski steps in the Antarctic. Relaxed is the key." Oh dear. It was hard to be relaxed when I didn't want to appear like a pathetic old granny in front of everyone. We all stepped into the skis and attached ourselves to the heavily loaded pulks by clipping to the traces.

Like horses in a chariot race, we were away. The only trouble was that the slowest horse, me, was put in the front of the 20 other horses.

We crept up a little hill and successfully negotiated a flat bit, only to find the gradient then went down the other side. Well, here we go, no shortage of gliding, pick up speed, much more chariot race like, help, really haven't got the hang of these skis at all, the weight of the pulk is pushing me from behind, wonder how I slow down, wham! I fell over. Couldn't get up with skis on and, wham! Wham! Wham! Major pile-up. After the disentangling, I wasn't asked to go in front again. So much for that chance to prove myself.

At the end of the training, Norway did give me one more chance. We were taken to a large lake below the tree line, where clumps of spindly birches waited out winter. Here the military had agreed to put us through their ice-break drill – so kind of them. If it wasn't for the flatness of the terrain it would have been easy to miss the fact that this was a lake, there was just so much snow-cover over the whole of the landscape. Sleet was blowing sideways and the sky was heavy with more snow on the way casting a sombre grey veil on the occasion. In the middle of the lake, a large hole had been sawn through the heavy ice revealing the blackness of unknown depth with ice fragments floating around in it. The idea was to put skis on, jump in one end, swim across and climb out the other.

No way!

My blood froze merely looking at it. It was scary, yes, but even scarier was the thought of being the only one not doing it. Sometimes things just have to be done. We pared down our clothes to thermals and windproof jackets and trousers, and then queued up. I wished I wasn't so near the back. The waiting was agony. One by one those in front fell, dived or somersaulted into the icy jaws, amid encouraging shouts and cheers, then climbed out with a variety of unusual expletives.

Every bit of my body was shaking. "I'm really worried about losing my contact lenses," I said to no one in particular. I couldn't take them out as it would mean I could barely see. But with them in there was a high chance of losing them. In fact, I was really worried about putting my head in at all. Then I put up my hood, which couldn't possibly help but made me feel better, poured my feet into the soggy boots provided, raised my arms to have a rope tied around and lightly strapped on the skis which were also on ropes. The moment of truth had arrived. I waddled to the edge. Somewhere in my mind was the memory of a quotation about being on the edge and flying... it was for courage... here goes.

I slipped in, managing to keep my head mostly above water. Wham! The cold hit me like a knife. Then, a burning pain. Instinct took over, my brain unattached itself from the body. My arms and legs floundered across what seemed like 50 metres. The violent kicking lost one of the boots... I have to get out... I have to get out... there's eight minutes to get out and be dry... or die. Somehow I brought my hands down the sticks so I now had their two points to dig in and impossibly claw my body oh so slowly out, using only arm force and expert wriggling. I was determined not to need the rope. Yeah! I did it! Let's hear it for granny power!

It took 45 minutes of running to bring the circulation back to my feet.

I'd had enough of chances to prove myself. Just for the moment....

Quickening of the Heart

Okay, I had to admit, Norway's cold had toughened me up a little. But it highlighted the need to find considerably more strength at all levels.

Life had been so busy in the physical that I had neglected to spend quiet time with myself working on an inner level. I knew this was how to find strength. So I took time out to kneel on my meditation stool at home and focus on the stillness. I listened to something that had been niggling at me for a while. We must go to the Antarctic humbly and with respect. We should seek permission from the land itself.

I knew this was important. I always tried to remember to ask permission of a mountain before climbing it, of a tree before pruning it, or of a pebble before moving it. I felt it was a way of honouring the oneness of life. So I now pictured myself at the far end of the Earth and asked lovingly in my mind "Please Antarctica, may we come and bring Peace Messages?"

And I dreamed: *I am flying. The Earth is beneath me and with the spinning I am flowing further... further. The ground meets me decked in a carpet of snow. There is a scene of whiteness and light. I am greeted by tall pillars, glowing with a misty, eerie brilliance. They are shining beings of light. I am invited to bring sacredness and to stand with them.*

I felt connected, and this did give me a sense of harmony and strength that was to be useful in the strenuous days ahead.

I resolved to remember to keep listening to inner guidance so I started meditating whilst my body was on the move. This is not the standard method of finding inner stillness but it suited me, as exercising began to take up more and more time in my life. Walking, swimming and running were the most useful in this regard (not so good meditating whilst playing tennis).

Training, training, training was the first thing to think on opening my eyes every morning. We had 10 months to go. Fitness was the top priority. Pete's superhero body seemed to be able to go from nothing to long days without a problem. Mine took a huge amount of coaxing and persuading to push it beyond what it wanted to do. However, Pete was delighted that I was actually planning my fitness. Well, more being dragged along by circumstances, really, because I had signed up to run the London Marathon. This was a useful aim, but after my disastrous 24-hour waddle, I knew that I had to seriously build up running muscles if I wanted to be successful. I couldn't afford to take any more three-month recovery times.

The training had to continue with some form of daily exercise. I tried to run twice during the week and once at the weekend, gradually lengthening that one, with a rest day afterwards. At first my knees were acutely painful, but slowly became more manageable as the surrounding muscles built up. I worked through it only because I was raising funds for the Tibet Relief Fund on the marathon and my training for that was for the South Pole. I couldn't get much more of an incentive, I told myself, when the last thing in the world I wanted to do was take an achy stiff body out into the rain and cold and persuade tired legs to move.

I joined a great circuit training class and my fitness programme took a turn for the better. The main problem was how to fit that in, as well as three runs, two swims, two walks, an everyday yoga session and rowing machine work all into one week.

I was feeling quite pleased with myself. I had discovered that once the body was warmed up, aches and pains tend to disappear and only come back when exercising has stopped, so by then it's too late to file complaints. I'm not sure, though, how I would've survived without the supplements that our nutritional sponsors Mannatech gave us. My body loved all their products. And I liked the energy of service with which they were sent out into the world. They were natural food-quality glyco-nutrients and helped give us energy, ease the muscles and keep our bodies in excellent working order. This was quite something considering the stress that we were putting them under, a situation that was going to become worse.

Whatever the help, though, there was always going be pain. However, I knew my marathon suffering would be nothing compared to the multiple and ongoing suffering of the Tibetan people. During the last month there had been uprisings in Tibet. It seemed that peaceful marches led by brave Tibetan monks had taken place across the country, protesting against half a century of occupation, persecution and genocide. The Chinese authorities had responded with shooting into crowds, arbitrary arrests, unspeakable torture, disappearances and executions in a brutal crackdown. This was all being covered up, not only for the world but also for their own people, sensitive as they were to the forthcoming Olympics in Beijing. It made me angry and intensely sad. I couldn't hear the news without my heart bleeding.

It put things in perspective for me. If I were a Tibetan in Tibet and carried a Tibetan flag through the streets of Lhasa it could bring on me a seven-year gaol sentence, torture and the possibility of execution. However, in our land of free speech, I could carry a Tibetan flag through the streets of London. Yes, I would do this. It would help hold the profile of Tibet in the public eye after all the recent press.

So, in a buzz of nervous excitement I lined up with the other 35,300 runners for the start of the marathon. It was amazing to be in this sea of humanity facing the challenge, many wearing fun costumes, most raising funds for charity, sharing the resources of the world, making a difference. I had attached my flag to a tall bamboo pole sticking out of my rucksack. Whilst I was running, it streamed out behind and was nicely displayed, though it blew about all over the place in the wind and threw me with it. I hoped I wouldn't upset others coming behind me, or worse, be disqualified for having a sail. Around mile 16 I had a bit of a problem. I felt a yank and heard a muffled cry. Turning, I saw something struggling underneath it. "Oops. Sorry." The wind gathered pace so that the flag covered my face and I had to fight to be able to see who it was that I bumped into. "Oops. Sorry." The flag had wrapped itself round a white rabbit, a furry womble off-course, too.

When the knee pain set in, it was the cheering crowd that kept me going, and the thought of seeing Pete at the drinks station after the rain. But by the time I was floundering through a treacle-like agony of exhaustion it was the thought of helping Tibet that kept me going, of the children and the monks, starving and homeless, in sickness and longing for education. "I can do this; I can do this" became my mantra as sheer will power kicked in at mile 20. The legs had long since given up, barely part of my body which swam in a sea of nausea. I knew I couldn't give up; I had to keep running though everything was seizing up. "I can do this; I can do this," and I shook my cramping calves passing mile 25, praying that they would last a bit longer, hold the focus, as mile 26 swung into view... hang in there, as the yellow finishing line shimmered like a mirage... hang in there... hang in there Tibet... we are all here for you... the flag pole scraping under the final arch. Retching and dazed, I was there...YES! You can run the distance.

Pete had wanted me to run in six hours. I just made it. The winner took around two hours.

I knew now, for sure, that endurance is a mind game. That things are possible if you have an incentive that is important enough to you.

But endurance had more training tricks up its sleeve.

Three days after the marathon, my body was able to walk again. Walk... ah... now there's a thought. According to Pete's fitness programme it was time to do a long walk. Sounds nice. Anything but running.

"What sort of distance did you have in mind?" I asked him.

"Er, 630 miles actually."

"630 miles!"

"Yes, you see, if we do a good walk, then our minds will know that this is quite possible. So when we're confronted with only walking 500 miles across the Antarctic it'll seem like a cinch."

"Ah..."

"That's the length of the South West Coast Path, Britain's longest national trail. We'll begin at Minehead in Somerset and go round to Poole harbour in Dorset."

My definition of a good walk wasn't quite the same as Pete's (but I wouldn't want to be a couch potato, would I?).

On the way to the start we made a diversion to the Albert Hall in London where we joined thousands of others to listen to the Dalai Lama. In his address he reminded us that we are all, each and every person, responsible for the Earth in that we are responsible for the peace, beauty and harmony of our own path. That we can contribute to creating a peaceful Earth by finding our own inner peace.

There were times, when we were pushing ourselves over the English countryside, when our path certainly wasn't harmonious.

One morning Pete was agitated. "Why d'you always take so long to get out of the tent? This is a training exercise. We have to be fast and efficient. You won't be able to faff around like this in the Antarctic."

I was taking even longer than usual as I was grappling with an eye infection caused by sleeping in my contact lenses. "If you don't chill out, you'll blow up," I retorted.

That was the day he had the palpitation. Then 70 miles further on another one that continued for much of the day. On each occasion he drank lots of water and in a weakened state, managed to keep going heroically, even on uphill stretches. We hoped that maybe his body was becoming used to dealing with palpitations. But the Antarctic was always in the back of our minds. There would be much more pressure there and we were going to be in life-threatening situations far from civilisation. Always we would wonder, how will we cope if a palpitation happens on the way to the South Pole?

By the third week of walking, our bodies, though always hungry, had become fitter and more efficient. So we found that they sweated less and were able to cope on less water (and were less smelly). Even so, there were many mornings when we would wake up exhausted, confronting the thought of shouldering a heavy rucksack and dragging sore feet along on legs empty of energy. It was then that the beauty of the way quietened the weary and complaining body. For the sea danced with the land creating a path of magnificent coastline views, holding the taste of seaweed on the ocean wind; and the sky hung a festival of seabirds strumming the plaintive song of the gulls. We were also encouraged by the people we met. "Have you come far?" asked one man out looking for old fossils. "Oh, about 550 miles." This prompted, "I'll suggest the wife does that..."

We completed the South West Coast Path by walking an average of 22 miles per day. We finished with a close hug born of battles fought side by side, and thanked the angels of the path for holding us safe. My kind-hearted sister Melanie came and took us back to her house for the one thing that we craved more than anything in the world – a hot bath.

It had been a good test of our resolve. In spite of trials and tribulations, we had shown our bodies and minds that it was okay to walk for 14 hours a day, to relentlessly march for a month with no rest days, that things that sound impossible work if you decide to do them, hold the focus, know you can do them, walk through the walls and – well – just do them.

Great. Only returning home, Pete discovered that on top of all his heart problems he also had a nasty abdominal hernia.

Not that it made any difference. He was continually reminding me, "We are training for the toughest race on

Earth. Yes, our bodies have been able to keep going for a month on the coast path, the muscles have developed and our level of fitness is good, but it's crucially part of an upward trend, so there's no sitting about resting now. We have to hold what fitness we've achieved and build on it."

Annoyingly, if I didn't exercise every day now, my body became stiff and seized up. So, soon after our long walk, I agreed to tackle something new – the Welsh 3,000s. This is an interesting day out in the mountains of North Wales. The challenge is to climb all of Snowdonia's 15 peaks that are over 3,000 feet high. The challenger has to climb up and down mountains over a distance of 33 miles. If that sounds too easy, then it's important to remember that it has to be achieved within 24 hours. It is a task undertaken by the young and the mentally deranged.

Following the principal that impossible can become possible when broken into bite-sized pieces, the route was divided into three sections. We began (with a group from the young category) in a wet misty dawn scrambling up and clambering along jagged knife-edge ridges, then repeatedly over heart racingly steep mountain slopes with knee-crunching descents. In the middle of the second section we crossed magnificent windswept summits perched on a fold of the Earth as though scampering along the back of a dragon and then slid down a loose scree slope. It was here that I noticed Pete was unusually slow and quiet.

"Is it a palpitation?" I asked, dreading the consequences.

He nodded and I imagined the churning inside that he was coping with. For someone with such go-for-it energy, a finish-the-job attitude and the importance of our training programme, this was the ultimate in frustration. He had to miss doing the last section.

For me the mind came into play taking me onwards, ever

onwards, with worn-out legs and uncomfortable eyes from dried out contact lenses in the incessant wind. By the time we reached the last summit the night was completely black. Only the little beams from head torches showed the slippery rocks and bogs and finally the beaten track of the way down, hour after timeless hour, until we reached a gathering dawn.

I had been very slow, but moving continuously across mountains for 23 hours had been good training. In spite of the inevitable physical exhaustion I felt that I had kept my vital energy throughout. There's a first for everything. It was a positive fitness indicator. From then on, I lost that sense of fighting against myself and began working *with* myself. Unfortunately, all this was overshadowed by the worry about Pete.

The disappointment and the apparent increase in the frequency of the palpitations prompted him to visit the cardiologist again. Drugs were prescribed. Was there a chance that something might actually slow him down? Hmm... unlikely. He spoke with the insurers again who confirmed that he would still be covered in the Antarctic, but not for three months after his forthcoming hernia operation. There was just time to fit that in.

We didn't need any more reminders of getting older, with dragging bodies that were falling to bits. Nor of the enormity of what we were tackling at our ages. But time passes. I became an old fuddy-duddy and was given a bus pass as I reached my 60th birthday. My sister Cathie generously organised a surprise party. I was the first to know about it and then the surprise became that so many people were actually able to make it. It was good to feel supported and loved by so many family – a springboard of security from which to jump off into the deep end of life. Amongst all the comings and goings of the gathering there were special moments with my little eight-month-old granddaughter Elsie. How can one little being inspire so much love, I wondered? Was it her complete trust, or excitement at the discoveries that life brings, or the joy at the sight of loved ones?

Meanwhile, the South Pole Race time-machine we were

riding moved up a gear. There was a press launch at the Ice Bar in London. Peace Messages were collected at local events. We moved reluctantly into mortgages and loans to cover the race fees. We walked for a couple of days – 65 miles around the Isle of Wight to get some exercise. We arranged to talk at schools about Peace Messages. South Pole Race sent us to Kaprun in Austria for crevasse-rescue training. At last, here we practiced a method that we could feel happy about. After setting up an anchor in the snow and a rope system with pulleys, I was able to haul up a heavier body by myself. The secret ingredient was to use leg power for the hauling. For the moment, worries about crevasses could wait. We were distracted by the Olympics in Beijing, the sadness for the Tibetans not allowed to represent Tibet, but also by the enthusiasm surrounding the athletes and the inspiration of pushing oneself to the utmost of human ability. Time was becoming closer for our own test. My excitement was rising.

Life was about to become more entertaining, as it was time to start pulling tyres.

Out on the Pull

If you're a friendly sort looking for a nice way of meeting people, I recommend taking a tyre for a walk. I don't know why it is, but the simple act of attaching an old car tyre to a piece of rope and dragging it along behind you suddenly makes you friends with everybody you see. It's quite extraordinary.

First you have to obtain your tyre. Garages are delighted that someone actually wants old tyres, they may even pay you to take them away, so you're likely to end up with a whole family, large and small. Then it's a good idea to put in a hole or two. If you're like Pete and do everything properly you can drill a hole for a bolt in one side and the same on the opposite side, making it possible to pull two tyres when you're feeling like Superman. More holes are useful to let the water out when you go through puddles or the sea, but this is quite an advanced technique.

So, attach one end of a two-metre rope to the tyre and the other end to something on yourself. The something can be a rucksack or a climbing harness. We use pulk harnesses. Two pieces of rope attached either side of the body leading back to the main rope give a better pull distribution. It's a good idea to think about the jarring effect on your body when your tyre gets stuck on something like an old stump, whilst you keep going. So a length of bungee in the rope helps put some "give" in the system.

And there you have it – an expert pulling machine. You'll be pretty hot, so put on shorts and a big smile then head out for your walk. We always use ski-sticks, but they're not essential. It's just that they help to simulate a good pulk-pulling motion.

At first I found that it was quite tricky to cope with being friends with everyone when I went out on the pull. I didn't know what to say to guys whose opening lines were "Aren't you tired out yet?" or "I could've carried that for you" or "Get a dog, it's a lot easier." And some were a bit strange, like the army sergeant who jumped out at me from behind a bush with "Have you got legal tread on that tyre?" or the driver who turned round to come back and tell me "You've got a puncture." After a while, I became better at just smiling sweetly and producing sponsor forms.

Kids were easier to deal with. They would always ask, "Why're you pulling that tyre?" I would reply, "I'm training to walk to the South Pole, so I'm practicing on pulling the pulk," and they would say "Cool! Can I come too?" Hmm... I wonder how many kids it would take to pull a pulk?

Dogs and horses were a bit more of a problem. They were pretty doubtful about the breed of dog that I was taking for a walk. This prompted barkings and prancings and commotions, whilst all I was doing was trying to go for a quiet walk...

Like all my fitness routines, I tried to start slowly and build it up. I pulled one light tyre for a little way, then gradually increased distance, number of times in the week and weight on the tyre. Like all his fitness regimes, Pete decided to go all-out immediately and started off by pulling up the beach from Southwold to Lowestoft and back, a distance of 22 miles. This was, of course, worthy of my superhero.

It was easy to fit tyre-pulling into general life. I pulled to visit friends, to go shopping, to the swimming pool, to circuit training; it was just a matter of parking the tyre outside. I began to feel naked if I went without one. And there's no doubt it was great training. It put together all our hard work of the year – the running, the long-distance walking, the climbing, the daily workouts. We were now building up muscles of the shoulders and back, triceps, biceps, stomach, thigh and calves. And maintaining the flexibility in the ankles. Our bodies were becoming fine-tuned machines for pulling pulks.

Any training break came as quite a shock to the system. For Pete, this happened because he had to have his hernia operation. I went to pick him up afterwards from the hospital, apprehensive about how I would find him. He was lying down looking dreadful. It took him a few minutes to be able to actually sit upright and show me the dressing over the long cut in his tummy. He was in a lot of pain and could barely move. Oh dear, I thought, it looks like these things take a lot of recovering from.

"Goodbye, Mr Hammond," the discharging nurse said, helping him out of the building. "Remember to take it really easy for at least four weeks."

"Some hope," I muttered under my breath.

In two weeks, he was back running every day and shortly afterwards back into full training.

Whilst Pete was meant to be slowing down, it seemed a good time for me to do some major body enhancement work and have an operation, too. I had been agonising for a whole year about whether to have my eyes lasered. All my life I'd struggled with extreme short-sightedness and bad astigmatism. My options in the harshness of the Antarctic environment didn't look good. To wear contact lenses could mean uncomfortable eyes – particularly in the wind – the freezing of lenses and lens solutions, the likelihood of eye infections and the impossibility of fiddling about with lenses with big gloves or frozen fingers. Wearing glasses would mean hopeless vision with misting up goggles, as well as an unworkable situation in the tent dealing with the steam coming from melting snow.

It was now or never for my own operation. I went to have laser vision correction surgery with Accuvision who are at the leading edge of this technology. They said I could do one eye at a time, as a way of being cautious, just in case. But there was no time for caution. The corneas of both eyes were reshaped by a precision laser beam. It was pretty scary. It was an intense experience. But I woke up the next morning being able to see without lenses or glasses for the first time in my life. It felt like a miracle.

The trauma hit me three days later. I became stressed, irritable and impatient. One eye was sore and my near vision hadn't settled down. I wondered if I'd done the right thing. Also, my body was missing the training. "No strenuous exercise for a week," I had been told. I hadn't even dared ask if tyre-pulling counted as strenuous.

My eyes soon healed, though the fine-tuning on reading small print was to take a few weeks. It wasn't long before I knew that the laser surgery was definitely the best thing I could've done. I worked out that the 10 minutes I was saving on not putting contact lenses in and out every day was around four days per year, or 160 days in the rest of my life. That's a lot of life to save and make the most of. It spurred me on. Tyre-pulling was back on the agenda.

Amazingly, the universe conspired to provide a friend who also had tyre-pulling on her list of things to do – Rima, tall and slim with a timeless beauty and a go-for-it attitude. We got on well immediately. She had contacted us to ask if we'd carry a special children's flag to the South Pole on behalf of the Gesar Foundation. This is a charity named after a brave and fearless 11th century Tibetan spiritual warrior, just like Pawo who runs it. Its purpose is to help the children of the world to be free from suffering and inspire them to see that all things are possible. Earlier this year, Rima had taken the Gesar flag to the North Pole. Yes, of course we'll try and fly it now at the South.

We went for a tyre-pull together around the Pen Y Fan horseshoe in the Brecon Beacons. Up and over wild mountains, dragging our tyres up impossibly steep slopes, in thick mud and nearly blown to oblivion by the harsh wind. It rained the whole way. We were soaked to the skin, but spent the day laughing. It was good to have three. It changed the dynamics of everything. Maybe Rima could join our team?

All our other friends had declined. It wasn't only for lack of cash. It appeared that many had heard the tale of the polar traveller who had failed to do up his flies and suffered frostbite in uncomfortable parts.

Maybe Rima?

We trained together with tyres around Windsor Park and Richmond Park. Then graduated to double tyres. "To the South Pole and beyond!" I practised our battle cry, puffing and panting whilst Rima glided effortlessly ahead.

"C'mon Tess, put more oomph into it," she called. "The work you do now is crucial. It'll pay off. It's like Chinese cooking. It's all in the preparation."

She should know, yes, for Rima is Chinese. Now I had a Chinese soul sister.

To increase the difficulty, we tackled pulling on steep hills while running and on the shingle beaches of Suffolk. I found this bordered on the impossible until discovering the secret of holding momentum. Then there was pulling up and down the sand dunes of North Devon. This excellent training ground was discovered accidentally, having been cut off by a fast, incoming tide. The only technique possible was to abandon sticks and crawl on all fours. My favourite training was pulling tyres along the beach whilst pushing the pram directed by a little bouncing Elsie shouting "whoirreeee" (for those who don't speak baby that's "Faster Granny! Faster!").

To portray a great image when out on the pull, use two tyres. The extra weight means more pressure from the harness onto the body. This compacts any recently devoured food in the stomach, like one of those can-crushers. My tummy tends to object, not unnaturally, by throwing up. This really doesn't look good. So I took to wearing my harness on the hips, which works better. The other problem with pulling two tyres is that the end one often gets out of control. So it's particularly hazardous passing people along narrow paths, negotiating steps or trying to avoid dogpoo. One day I thought I'd cracked it. I had a well-behaved end tyre that wasn't holding me up at all, until I discovered that it had dropped off and hidden in a ditch a good mile back. I would have to be more aware of my load in the Antarctic.

Towards the end of October, Pete and I decided to undertake a tyre-pull of a reasonable length – the 105 miles of the South Downs Way, from Eastbourne to Winchester. If we could complete this we would set a new world record. It had never been done before. This sounded a worthy item to have on our 100-years-old-life-achievement list. It had the added interest of drawing some publicity. Local papers produced headlines such as "Granny Goes Out on the Pull" and "Here's What to Do When You Retire."

We tied on a tent and sleeping bags to slats that were attached to the tyres, shouldered our rucksacks and set off. Even though we'd recently had more than our fair share of adventures, there was that wonderful feeling of excitement, the anticipation of the unknown and the familiar feeling of life on the trail. By the second day, there was also that other now-too-familiar feeling – of disaster. Pete had a palpitation again. This one came and went within half an hour. But then he had another one, and this one wouldn't stop.

We sat in a pub and discussed the situation. "I cannot go to the South Pole like this," he said wretchedly, taking his wrist pulse with his fingers and needlessly checking the time on his watch again and again. No, his pulse was still racing madly. The palpitation had not stopped. "They're occurring more often now. I never know when one will happen, or when it'll stop, or even if I'll need hospital treatment to make it stop. I can't take the risk of one happening on the ice. If one comes, then our only option is to stop and put up the tent. But if there's a blizzard or we're dealing with falling down a crevasse or we're both exhausted or with numb or even frostbitten fingers, what then? The chances are that we wouldn't be able to cope. It's not fair on you to go with this sort of a risk."

I knew what hurt most of all. He didn't want to let either of us down.

My heart clenched. The ramifications of him not going were unthinkable. Probably it would scupper the whole trip for both of us, as I couldn't go by myself. We'd been in this situation before. All the months of training and preparation, all the money committed and most important of all, the Peace Messages...

What could we do about it? Pete had been eaten up with worry for weeks. He had tried two different sessions of drugs. Neither had made the slightest difference. However, he had seen the cardiologist again last week and was told that an operation known as a catheter ablation was something that might work. It could be done on the NHS, but the chances of taking place in our timescale were slim. Have it done when you get back from the Pole, was the recommendation, but waiting was not an option.

"I think I'll have to do the operation, but privately," he said. "Wrecking this tyre-pull is the last straw. Trouble is, it'll cost £6,000 which I don't have. I'll have to try and take out yet another mortgage. I won't be insured for the race, but if the South Pole Race can accept that, then I'll have to take the risk too. It's the only answer. We'll just have to hope that I can get a date that leaves some recovery time before we go. Assuming it works, of course."

A dark cloud settled over me. I tried to stay calm. But everything in me seemed to be shaking in a state of shock and disbelief. If he had the operation there were still no guarantees; we knew of two people for whom it didn't work. Even if it did work, we couldn't get away from the fact that it wasn't too clever having major heart surgery just before crossing the Antarctic in the toughest race on Earth.

In the Lap of the Gods

Pete's heart operation was set for 17th November, exactly four weeks before leaving for the South Pole. Would my superhero get through all this? Well, if anyone could, he could. We would just have to trust, relax and believe that all was well. There wasn't too much relaxing to be had, though.

After the palpitations stopped and the medical procedure was being sorted out, it was business as usual. In typical fashion Pete said, "C'mon. We've got to finish the tyre-pull." Nerves of steel. How could he stay so calm through all of this? He had analyzed the problem, made a decision, acted on it and then moved on. I was still a nervous wreck. With only a day's break we set off again from where we'd left off. I gratefully allowed myself to be rocked back into a peaceful state by the beauty and steadfastness of the Earth, over which we pulled our tyres. The Downs rolled before us, decked in open farmland and gentle autumn tones, giving us a variety of mud, puddles, stones and high piles of crunchy leaves. Happily, we felt able to cope with whatever confronted us.

In spite of the problems, we completed the tyre-pull in six and a half days, which meant an average of 16 miles per day. This was not far short of the basic distance that we would need to achieve in the Antarctic. Our bodies now accepted 10-hour days on the move as normal. Importantly, we needed no recovery time and were able to return straight into our everyday training. We knew that our raised fitness would mean better tolerance to cold weather exercise and increase our capacity to perform. This would generate heat more efficiently, hopefully keeping us warmer. Pete grumbled about my speed (well, his legs are much longer...) but I was really pleased with the way my fitness was progressing. I just had to continue to keep on top of it. What did worry me, though, was how bad my skiing had been in Norway.

One day Rima said, "I know, let's go roller skiing. It'll help your technique on the snow."

We went to a roller-skiing circuit, the non-snow equivalent to cross-country skiing. We put on elongated skates with wheels, helmets, knee pads, elbow pads and a big smile, the last of which wiped off as I staggered round, struggling to keep my balance. "Good arm position," I was told when it became apparent that that was the only thing which was likely to be any good. "Think about the glide. Try and swing the hips, body static, weight on the balls of the feet, focus pressure on alternate legs." I was too busy concentrating on staying upright. Eventually, I managed to reach a brave steady speed with the semblance of a drunk penguin. Why does it always take so long for an old body to adopt new thinking? At the age of 21, I had only to suggest a new way of doing something and my body would respond immediately with "Okay let's do it." Now it took a heap of badgering to even get "Did you say something?"

So, that was roller skiing. "Yeah," Rima giggled. "You obviously need more time to perfect the technique." But time was running out. In fact, time on the snow would be the most useful.

But this along with everything else hung in the balance. It all depended on Pete.

The day of the operation was cloudy and chilly, mirroring how I felt inside. I was so nervous I felt physically sick. He'd been told the previous night that there was no bed for him. Hopefully they would do it today after all. Arriving at Papworth Hospital near Cambridge, I read the sign on the gate: "The UK's largest specialist cardiothoracic hospital." That sounded positive. It took me an inordinately long time to find where he was. Eventually, I tracked him down. He was sitting in a waiting room ready to go home, in his usual let's-get-on-with-it state. I couldn't believe it. I had expected the wreck that I had picked up after the hernia operation, but I had my superhero. Admittedly one taking a day off, but that was no bad thing.

"Success," he beamed with a hug. "I've had the top cardiologist. They stuck two wires up the veins in my groin and burnt the abnormal heart tissue with high-frequency electrical impulses. Apparently I had two faults done for the price of one. No wonder they were playing up. I can't lift anything for a week, nor drive, but I've been cleared to go."

I knew what he meant. He'd been cleared to go to the South Pole. Wow, the wonders of modern medicine! The process had been a high shock to his body, however, and more specifically to his heart. There was no telling how this would affect a body being pushed to limits.

As we left, the nurses said, "Now take it gently. Don't overdo it." Yeah. Right. But it seemed to me they treated him with awe. I suppose not too many 62-year-old patients come in for major heart surgery hoping it'll make them fit enough to go to the South Pole.

Four hectic days later Pete, Rima and I climbed on board a plane to Finland, with pulks, skis and a tent, changed planes at Helsinki and found ourselves right on the Arctic Circle, at Rovaniemi. This was the capital of Lapland. Happily, the temperature was minus 10°C – a winter wonderland. Lovely. Our footsteps were crunchy on the snow as we walked along what had previously been a river before being swallowed up by ice chunks. The trees were made of white crystal and the ice knives were out in the air attacking unwary ears and fingers. Magic was floating down from all around in a softness that only new snow can bring, speaking of an eternal "now". It was what we needed. We spent a happy week wandering across a national park in the snow and cold, becoming used to the gear and the skiing. I never did reach the natural slide-and-glide state of the skiing. Ah well, teaching old dogs and grannies new tricks an' all that...

We had worked well as a team of three and still had hopes that Rima would come south with us. She was trying to find a way to do it and promised to give us a definite decision soon. It was amazing that someone had the strength of character to even think about it at this late stage, but that was Rima.

During our stay in Lapland, the sky remained heavy and it had snowed on and off for the whole time. We had longed for clear weather to be able to see the Northern Lights (Aurora Borealis). Along with the Southern Lights (Aurora Australis), these are natural light displays visible in the night sky, named after the Roman goddess of dawn, Aurora. They are caused by the interaction between the Earth's magnetic field and the solar wind – a wild party of highly charged particles. Some early peoples believed this to be the "Dance of the Spirits".

In my memory was a story that spoke of the Auroras as the regions of the sky where the veils between the worlds are thinnest and one can pass through to a different world, *if* one can reach the deep core of one's being.

We hadn't seen the mysterious Northern Lights, though I felt sure that they were there. Clouds and daylight wouldn't stop them happening. They would just be invisible to us. But hey, we were team Southern Lights and in a couple of weeks we would be at the other end of the Earth, at home with the "Dance of the Spirits".

Wings of the Messenger

Soon after returning from Lapland, team Southern Lights was given an assignment, one we knew was of the utmost importance for our work of helping the peace and harmony of the Earth.

On previous peace climbs we had placed a quartz crystal in each zone whilst sending off the Peace Messages. The purpose of the crystals had been to hold, amplify and transmit the energy of the Messages. Each one had been programmed to the same frequency. I could see now that this was creating the star of peace across the Earth. So it had been like fixing the star with little beacons of light.

We had been guided on these occasions by Master Advarr, an ascended spirit master, channelled by Ivy Smith. Together they lovingly work for the higher consciousness of Divine energy and the healing of the planet. Now, for the South Pole assignment, we were advised:

"...We will supply you, my child, with another crystal, but we will also give you a grid to work with because this signal is going to be the major shift energy and this is why it will be your greatest and hardest task. There will in the centre [of the circular grid] be a rose quartz crystal, because love is what the Earth needs and the vibration of each person upon it. But around the crystal itself will be citrine. We will give nine citrine crystals, nine being the completion number. Then, my child, there will also be a small double terminated clear quartz crystal which will give the shift *energy... This crystal and its grid will be very profound. It will begin to make a very big difference to the Earth itself... It is for the golden age...*

You will be guided onwards. Fear will be overtaken by the great challenge and the knowing within your soul that you have to fulfil these things..."

Our task, it seemed on this occasion, was to place a job-lot of crystals at the South Pole.

A brown padded envelope came in the post, warm from the postman's van. Inside I could feel a strong clear energy of coldness as though I held in my hand a bag of ice. I was getting powerful whooshes up and down my spine. The crystals had arrived.

I stared at them, mesmerised. There was a rose quartz pebble of a delicate pink which seemed to touch me at a deep heart level with tenderness; nine shiny pebbles of golden citrine catching the light in dancing flashes; and a double-ended clear quartz with a sense of movement and flow.

I laid them in a circle with the rose quartz – the stone of love – in the centre. Then lit candles, chanted an "OM" and visualised them in the ice at the South Pole. They held a beautiful sense of presence. Then I packed them away in a sacred black Tibetan bag embossed with gold together with other precious items to take: the complete printout of all the Peace Messages; some of the children's original Messages; a tiny camera chip holding photos of all the Peace Messages; and a small Tibetan flag. To further enhance the peace energy I included a candle burnt with the essence of the World Peace Flame and a picture of the Dalai Lama.

We had also been sent a pack of nine extra citrine crystals. I forwarded eight off to friends around the world who were to be a wider support circle, holding and strengthening the energy for peace. We were to hold the ninth.

The plan was that, at the end of January 2009, Ivy's group at the Wattle Centre in London would hold a six-day vigil as an anchor for the star of peace. Meanwhile, we would have a ceremony in the Antarctic to activate the crystals. At 9pm GMT on 29th January, there was to be the main peace ceremony with people all round the world tuning-in whilst we, as near as possible to this time, spoke out the Peace Messages and laid the crystals in a resting place within the ice.

We knew that from our point of view any plan would be subject to all sorts of changes and unknowns due to the extreme conditions. We had gone for the 29th as Tony had told us that, all being well, the 30th was the last day possible to fly out of the South Pole back towards home. It was impossible to give a definite date as anything might happen, but we had sent far and wide the invitation for people to join with us in their thoughts for peace on the 29th. Now all we could do was trust, relax and believe that somehow it would all come together.

The crystals had been programmed for the peace and harmony of the planet to the same frequency as those in our other zones of the Earth, which were making up the star of peace. I had been entrusted with the crystals as the guardian messenger. Yes, we would do whatever was asked of us to deliver them to the South Pole.

All we had to do was cross the Antarctic...

Holding the Nerve

The thought of taking the crystals and the Messages to help the Earth gave me readiness of mind about our overall purpose. This confidence was boosted by the knowledge that I was the fittest that I had ever been. At the age of 60 this was a good thing, even though it had taken many long, slow months of build-up. It showed that training and hard work ultimately do win through. Of course my strength would be nothing compared to that of all the others on the race who were younger and nearly all male, but at least I knew that I had done the best that I could.

I had a huge problem, however, with translating this confidence into the practicalities of preparation. I rushed about trying to do lots of things at once, doing none of them properly. My energy was here, there and everywhere. This meant that I couldn't think rationally and focus on the job at hand. The thought that kept attacking me was, "There's so much to do and I'll never be ready". I had trouble switching it off. It was as though I wanted the bigger picture to happen so much that I lost looking after myself. I loved the collecting of the Messages and all that that entailed, but the preparation of the kit was really stressing me out. I had a room in the house piled with things to take, to sew, and adapt and pack, which – like my mind – never seemed to become ordered. I knew the basis was that I was excited, and the time was drawing nearer. Adrenalin was pumping around my body ready for fight or flight. Yes, I did need adrenalin, but not so much yet, please. Finally I had to admit it. The stress was being exacerbated by fear. I was downright terrified.

Some days it just took a hold of me. I was okay whilst training (there must be something about physically working the body that helps), but then it would sneak up on me unannounced and I would find myself shaking. I even gave up taking my pulse as a way of monitoring fitness, as I was getting crazy readings. Once I'd admitted the fear to myself, it was a little easier to cope with; then it was possible to admit it to others. That helped even more as everyone was so supportive. Friends told me to calm down; bring my energy down to my stomach level; nurture my inner self; be present in the moment; ground myself; concentrate on my breathing; that it is possible to go quickly without rushing. How often it seems easier for others to see answers that one can't see oneself.

Maureen at circuit training gave me the homeopathic remedy, Soul Support, to try. One day I measured my blood pressure and pulse. It was a sky-high 166/108 – 58. Then I took the remedy and did another reading. It had settled to 128/80 – 52. The difference was astounding. I used Soul Support often after that and felt it helped to calm me. I like homeopathy and things that work with the body rather than against it. I also like the idea that a tiny essence of something positive, even if physically unquantifiable, can make a difference on a larger scale – such as one little person doing something positive and making a difference around the Earth. This thought was a light that shone on the shadow of the fear.

Pete and I sent emails to each other in amongst the preparation fever:

"All is well. Love you."

He saw things differently, telling me, "Whatever is there to be scared about? Everything's taken care of. You'll be fine. Get yourself ready. Work from a list. Do one thing at a time."

I was grateful for his straightforward strength, but replied, "I don't know what it is. Maybe that it's all so huge... so unknown, so cold. I can't quite put my finger on it. It's a sort of instinctive fear."

A nervous stomach tied up in knots was causing havoc with my eating, even of bananas, my staple diet. I couldn't seem to shove in enough food and I was meant to be fattening up. We would expect to lose a lot of weight in the Antarctic, and extra fat keeps the body warm. Dom at my favourite health food shop suggested taking kelp to increase my appetite. "Oh, and it's also great for growing beards," he said (Dom's so clever at fulfilling the needs of his customers).

We had been told to try and put on two stone in weight, one stone of muscle and one of fat. I thought that with a smaller body I could get away with less, but still it was a lot to try for. I had managed about half a stone of muscle with all the fitness training, but I couldn't seem to put on any more weight; the continual exercise was making it impossible. In fact, in the past couple of weeks I had actually been losing weight. I tried to eat little and often all day which helped the low-blood sugar levels I was getting when exercising. Oh dear, I wasn't meant to be depleting the body yet. I tried to fatten up with things that I didn't normally eat, like butter and cream, but my stomach objected. I was very aware of the needs of my body, but it was a what-I-need-now sensitivity. Stocking up for times of famine didn't seem to be in the remit. Pete reckoned he was eating so much that his stomach was actually swearing at him.

As the final days before departure zoomed along in a hectic cloud, nervousness exploded into a kind of wild excitement. I was in a weird state that felt like I was flying about above my head. I couldn't eat. I couldn't sleep. Support from family and friends helped me find a sane path through it all, especially from my sons. Scottie told me, "Just remember, Mum, you've chosen to be where you are. You're doing exactly what you want to do, more than anything in the world."

"Yes, I do know. Thank you."

Marco told me, "Stay on mission, Mum. Keep strong by holding onto why you're doing it."

"I shall stay on mission. Stay on mission..."

He and his lovely girlfriend Chloe came and did the

breakfast packs for us. We needed 40 for Pete and 40 for me. These were concoctions of seven powders designed for high protein, high energy and high glycol-nutrients to put on the morning's oats. The packs joined the 160 parcels of pills (six types) to be taken twice a day.

Paul texted from a retreat where there was no communication with the outside world:

> "Safe travels. Am here in spirit for you every step of the way."

I received it as I was on my way to a book signing in London's Oxford Street, passing a shop window which synchronistically displayed a large sign: "With you every step of the way."

I also took a day to walk on the Downs to practice with my GPS. This little instrument is meant to tell you exactly where you are in the world. I knew that I was so bad technically I couldn't use it to find my way out of the local supermarket. After some time, I felt happy that I would be able to find my way out of the supermarket in a blizzard. It had just taken some quiet moments by myself to get it – easy when you know how, like so many things.

One thing that really flustered me was the thought of going to the loo in the snow. It was alright for the men; they had the equipment. How was I going to negotiate a layer of thermals, a layer of fleece and the huge salopettes which required shoulder straps underneath a jacket to hold them up, all with layers of gloves on and without getting a frozen bum and losing heat? It sounded hopeless. I'd struggled with this before and we were going to be in even colder conditions. I spoke with Matty whilst she was making us some of her designer gaiters and gloves. "Put in through-the-crotch zips with long tags," she said, "for the thermals, just cut splits in them. Don't go for underwear." The whole process sounded rather draughty to me. But I acted on her advice. On a similar note, a friend gave me a Whiz, a kind of female adapter funnel for weeing in inconvenient places. Presumably the South Pole is classified as inconvenient. It seemed silly, but I chucked it in the "to go" pile.

Six days before departure, new boots arrived. Finally the Norwegian factory had managed to produce a different prototype. Should I use these? They were not as floppy as the old ones and had sturdy leather support which looked to be much better, but when I tried them with socks, felt liners and blue outer socks, nothing fitted together. The felt liners were too big, the outers too small and my toes rubbed on the front of the boot. In despair I went to see Jo, the local podiatrist. "Use your old floppy boots and take lots of super-cold glue," she advised. I could have hugged her. Decision made, panic over. I would just have to pray that the old boots didn't fall to bits. They would only have to walk 500 miles.

Another panic concerned the sewing, which seemed to be never-ending. My neighbour Justine helped me with making pockets all over the thermals, face-protector flaps to attach to the goggles and in redesigning a rucksack with outside pockets. Quite by chance she made a pocket that could be perfect for a tiny fluffy penguin. Ah, I just happened to have one named Empie in the freezer where he was on trial along with energy bars, toothpaste, face creams, foot creams, batteries – he was just the right size. That booked *his* seat to the South Pole.

What about Rima's? She phoned from Singapore where she was pulling a tyre on the annual marathon there. "I'm sorry, I've tried everything. I don't want to let you guys down, but I definitely can't make it. My last chance of raising the cash hasn't materialised."

"Thanks so much for trying, Ri."

"I'm counting on you guys to do it. Do it for peace and light. Stay focused, be patient with each other and efficient. Above all, have fun. To the South Pole and beyond. Yeah!"

That was it then. No third team member.

Tony said, "Okay. Two's fine."

He couldn't really say anything else, especially as we knew that the Norwegians, Stian and Rune, were coming as a team of two as well, but then they had the strength of youth to pull the team gear – tent, shovels, rope and stoves – a task usually shared by three. Another thing that bothered us about being only two was the safety angle. The thought of pulling Pete out of a crevasse on my own had me quaking at the knees. Then there was putting the tent up or down in gale force winds. The worry worm had plenty to feed on.

But then... the universe had conspired for it to be this way. Team Southern Lights was to be a team of two.

The Emperor

Finally the last day came; we were to leave early the following morning. Like the childhood memories of waiting for Christmas, it had always been impossibly in the future and now suddenly it was here. I was off to the South Pole. It was 14th December, the day nearly 100 years ago when Amundsen's party had become the first humans to be there, beating Scott by a month. Would history repeat itself, or could there be a British victory over the Norwegians? Or maybe with our Peace Messages it would be possible to spread a little light on a different race, where everyone is a winner – the race for the peace and harmony of our Earth. The victory of humanity over itself.

A courier knocked at the door to deliver camera batteries. A round friendly face greeted me. "Ah, ya neighbour said ya'd gone to South Pole." He spoke with a captivating Jamaican drawl.

"No, not until tomorrow."

"Gad thing ar checked. Why ya goin' to South Pole then?"

"We're going to take Peace Messages to help the Earth."

"Ah, cool man. Ya're one o' those Earth people then. Never thought ar'd meet one, ya knaw. Ya see 'em on TV." He beamed a huge delighted smile.

"Yeah, I guess..."

"Ya must like winter then."

"Well, not really – but it's got to be done," I smiled.

Cold Hands, Warm Heart

"Thanks so much, 'bye." Closing the door I felt such a sense of contentment. I had had the distinct impression that this stranger, like so many of the children who send in Messages, instinctively knew the value of helping the Earth in this way. That, without having to go into all the physics of how everything is interconnected in a "soup" of vibrations, sending out prayers of peace could actually contribute to bringing peace. Inexplicably, this little exchange had confirmed for me that what we were doing was really important. Somehow we were doing it for him, for all the people of the world.

This gave me some calm to savour the enormity of what we were trying to do. I managed to give up stressing about what to take, packed my pulk with what was in the "to go" piles and spent the last few hours recording the Peace Messages onto my MP3 player. I read them all with no names so they all flowed into each other like one huge outpouring prayer. Now we had a back-up, whatever happened in the Antarctic. If the written Messages were blown away into a crevasse – or we were – they could still be spoken out. The beauty of them, with their longing for a more peaceful world, stirred my heart. So many people who care, it filled me with hope.

I was grateful, as always, for the technical help of Mary. She was suffering from some lurgy, which she didn't want me to take to the South Pole, so we communicated about which MP3 buttons to press by speaking through the letter box on the front door. I would miss modern conveniences.

Pete was his usual organised self, never panicking; he had his list to tick off. He used up most of a roll of duct tape preparing the pulks, which aren't the easiest things to pack for a plane journey. We had to make them look empty and light, hoping that no one would look inside and see sleeping bags, duvet jackets, roll-mats, 80 energy bars, ice axe, fuel bottles... it was a bit like taking a canoe as hand-luggage.

Finally we were ready. Somehow we had some sleep. In the morning, we briefly lit a candle for blessings on the mission, said goodbye to the cats and walked out the door. On the way I grabbed Gaius, my impressive foot-high cuddly penguin.

"You're not taking *that*, are you?" Pete said, looking distinctly worried.

"Yes, why not?"

"Well, I've chucked out masses of vital equipment so as to keep our weight down, and you're taking a *penguin*!" The exasperated tone of his voice was rising.

"The Emperor penguin is the most altruistic animal on Earth. In the depths of the Antarctic winter they huddle together and take it in turns to be on the outside to keep everybody else warm. Survival of the individual depends on survival of the whole. It's such a lovely principal that Gaius represents – to bring with us. Anyway, we need another team member."

"Oh, my God. C'mon or we'll miss the plane."

I got away with it, but ran into a problem at Heathrow. Surprisingly, the pulks went through okay. Then at "bag control" my rucksack was taken away by stern looking officials who were muttering amongst themselves and looking at me. I was called over. "Is this yours?"

I nodded.

"Please unpack it all."

Oh no, they think I'm hiding something illegal in the penguins. In fact, I had taken the stuffing out of Empie to hide the Tibetan prayer flags in him and then sewn him up. I just hoped they wouldn't touch the crystals. Surely they wouldn't suspect a little old granny. But no, what they were most interested in was that I had a rucksack full of strange white powder neatly packed into six weekly bags. "What's all this?"

"Oh that... eh, that's Empact. It's a sports drink. You see I'm going to walk to the South Pole and it's to help me get there." They didn't believe me. No doubt they have troublesome grannies every day. They took away some of the powder, eventually returned it and let me go.

On the plane to South Africa, I thought there might be time for some quiet conversation with Pete. "How're you feeling?" I asked.

"Yeah, great," he replied and promptly fell asleep for the

entire journey. He can sleep anywhere. I studied his familiar face with loving concern. Yes, his brow was relaxed, the determined jaw was set beneath the beard, and the smiley lines were just as smiley as ever. He did look fine, but it was a miracle against all odds that he was here. It was only due to his amazing strength of will, I was grateful for that, but had his body recovered from the two major operations? Time would tell.

Before trying to sleep, I delved into my rucksack and pulled out the sacred bag. Holding it in my hands I felt the coldness of the crystals through the thin material, again with that strange sense of presence and sat with that feeling for a while. Hmm. Crystals magnify thought. That meant that, as the guardian messenger, whatever I thought would be magnified. I attempted to see the responsibility of this. I would somehow have to try and find the inner peace that the Dalai Lama speaks of, wouldn't I? Okay, I promise, to try and keep my heart warm, to try and keep positive with loving thoughts, so that I shall be in the right frame of mind and, more importantly, the right energy of unconditional love to let off the Peace Messages and to place the crystals. I will try and hold a giving spirit.

I snuggled down with my comfy penguin pillow and the plane droned on across the world.

Cape Town passport control was full of long queues of tired passengers. Eventually, I reached a booth where a large lady in uniform looked down at me through glasses perched on the end of her nose and held out her hand for my passport. Then, without saying a word, she indicated for me to give her what I was holding in the crook of my left arm – Gaius. I passed him over. Surely penguins were allowed into South Africa, apartheid had been banned for 14 years now.

The passport lady held Gaius tightly, returned my passport and waved me on. No, I wasn't going to go through without our third team member. I watched while she folded her rather plump limbs around him more securely and waved me on with a flick of her head. I waited. Passengers behind me were becoming restless. I would have to do something about this.

Luckily, the window between us was big enough for me to reach both arms through and make a grab. I would either get arrested or be able to retrieve Gaius, thankfully it was the latter.

It's all very well, but there are limits to this giving thing.

Cape of Good Hope

Once through immigration, it was good to gather and chat with all the other South Pole racers setting out on such an incredible adventure together. We were six teams and two film crews. We were met by the Warrior, who was wearing a tight T-shirt over bulging chest muscles and sporting a magnificent Mohican haircut.

"Hey, Warrior," I greeted him. How could anyone *not* call him a Warrior, looking like that?

"Warrior of light. Yeah! The Warrior of light never rushes, he always takes his time."

"Great sentiments for the start of a race." My opinion of the Warrior went up.

It wasn't until the pulks and mountains of luggage had been loaded and we were on the bus to the hotel that he said, "I see you have Tibetan flags on your bags. I flew the Tibetan flag at the North Pole this year in protest of the Chinese climb of Everest just before the Olympics." My opinion of him went higher. It was good to know that we shared some similar concerns. He was to lead all the teams up through the crevasse area on the acclimatisation leg, as well as making sure everyone was up to speed and looking after the safety before the race started. I felt we would be in good hands. I surreptitiously showed him the crystals and the Peace Messages. His eyes gleamed. "So you're upholding good British tradition by carrying rocks to the South Pole like

Captain Scott."

The road from the airport gave us enticing views of beautiful Table Mountain, standing proud as Cape Town's jewel with a backdrop of horizon-to-horizon blue skies. Today there was no sign of the tablecloth clouds which so often lie on the top and spill over towards this great city. Its history is steeped in wealth and sadness and is also a wonderful example of change towards humane politics with respect and opportunity for all types of people – a new world era upheld by Nelson Mandela. Yet I could see that there was still a way to go. We drove past acres of shanty towns, full of ramshackle shacks where poverty ruled, and then into a metropolis of skyscrapers. The imbalance of rich and poor, like that in the wider world, was extreme.

I suddenly felt guilty. I knew that our air-flight alone to the Antarctic and back was costing £15,000 each. That would feed an awful lot of people. Stay on mission, I heard in my mind. In 1910, Scott passed by the Cape of Good Hope aiming for the South Pole to further the knowledge of humanity. If we in 2008, passing by the Cape aiming for the South Pole, can help to raise the *consciousness* of humanity, then that is something to help everybody, rich and poor, in the longer term. I resolved to share our journey by writing about it on our return.

By an interesting synchronicity, both Scott's team and team Southern Lights happened to end up in a race, though neither wanted to race. Why was it that life had panned out like this, on the way to achieving our respective missions? I see synchronicities as pointers, as signposts along the way. So what was this one about? Was it perhaps the wider picture – that we were all, each and every one of us – in a race that we hadn't wanted to be in? Was it to do with the race for the peace and harmony of the planet?

We emerged into the city centre, streets full of the ghosts of lavish colonial lifestyles and drove down a beautiful, tree-lined avenue. Drawing up outside the building that was to be our home for two days, the Fountains Hotel, the Warrior pointed out a large plinth near the entrance, carved from grey stone. On the top was a bronze statue of an old ship, representing the *Terra Nova*, which had docked here in 1910. Engraved were the words:

> "In memory of Robert Falcon Scott RN who with four companions from the Terra Nova perished March 1912 in returning from the South Pole."

There was no getting away from it. Captain Scott was to haunt us whether we liked it or not.

I wondered if he would have had to put up with the same heat. We had prepared ourselves for cold, but here we were at *plus* 30°C. We sweltered. Normally I love this temperature, but now I found I only wanted to curl up in a cool corner inside the hotel, like a snail on holiday, and conserve energy. However, there were more pressing things to think about. We went straight into a meeting room for a military style rapid-fire briefing from Tony. My travel weary brain wasn't too pleased, but no doubt everyone in the other teams was feeling the same (though they all looked a bit too sprightly for me).

Tony went straight into the instructions for the next six weeks. There was only one proviso. Everything would probably change. I let it pass. Never mind the principle of impermanence – that all things are in a permanent state of flux; my brain wanted nicely laid out facts about how everything would be. It was a good thing that I didn't know then just how frustrating change was going to be.

The Warrior reminded us, "We are pioneers. Everyone said the race couldn't happen, but we're doing it." Well done, Tony and team for the drive and logistical brilliance in achieving it... so far.

Pioneers have to prepare for the times when there are no handy supermarkets. Food packing was the next and most crucial job. Pete and I were sharing a room, more like an apartment, with team Danske Bank – Christian, Gaz and Gary. When we all walked in, the central lounge area was piled high with boxes and packets that wouldn't have left much room in a standard sort of greenhouse. This was food for five of us for 40 days. We were tempted to sit down and laugh at the ridiculous thought of eating all this, but we had the time pressure of having to have it all sorted by noon the next day. By noon we needed to have 10 days' supplies in our pulks for the acclimatisation leg, 15 days' supplies in a bag for the first half of the race and 15 days' supplies in another bag for the second half. Hmm, 40 days and 40 nights in the wilderness. Maybe we were setting out for a time of deep listening.

The biggest problem was that we had no definite idea how much we were going to need. Food is basic fuel for everything in the body to work. All the experts had advised that long days of hauling in extreme cold could be expending up to 9,000 calories a day. The human body cannot physically absorb more than 5,000 calories a day, even if one had the time and desire to munch through more. Pete and I, with older bodies, wouldn't need as much as the youngsters. My requirements with a smaller body would be less than Pete's. Our normal tastes were likely to change, but to what? In a hot hotel room feeling relaxed and well fed, it was not easy to understand, in the days to come, how hungry we were to be or how important food was to become.

We did know that the weight that we had to pull was a vital consideration. Food is very heavy and would slow us down. In this respect, the less food the better. It was important to find the balance and not end up either intensely hungry or hauling vast amounts of unnecessary food across the Antarctic. We needed to get it right because we couldn't abandon anything or find any more, though at least there would be opportunities to leave rubbish at the two resupply places – the start of the race and the halfway checkpoint.

We decided that the right balance could be achieved from the what-looked-about-right method.

Breakfast for team Southern Lights was relatively simple. We decanted 40 plastic bags of oats, to be supplemented by our packs of powders. This was around 800 high-carbohydrate calories between us. The evening meals were in add-water-to-the-bag lots, so only needed some of the packaging cut off for us to have less to carry. These meals supplied 800 calories each, and the puddings 600 calories. We sorted them into 10 evening-meal packs. As South Pole Race had supplied these foods we had no idea what they would be like, but at least they had provided vegetarian for us. Also huge logs of cheddar cheese that we cut into ice-cube sizes. We had planned to take butter for extra fat, but that didn't seem possible to organise in the heat.

So, in theory, we had to supplement the two meals of the day with around 2,000 calories each of day-food. Pete went out with Gaz and Gary to buy nuts and chocolate. He came back with bright pink canvas shopping bags.

"Lovely bags," I said.

"Told you I'd score brownie points with the bags," Pete beamed to the boys.

"How much were our nuts and chocolate?" I asked.

"1,200 rand."

"1,200 rand! That's 90 quid! How can you spend *90 quid* on nuts and chocolate?" I ranted. Brownie points, like many good things in life, are ephemeral.

We divided the nuts into eight bags and the broken-up chocolate into 16 bags and started on the day-food packs. These had to be separate. Pete's needed twice as much as mine did, plus all the jelly-baby sweets. I wanted no sweets, but did want dried fruit. The bulk of our day food was muesli and energy bars, which gave a good balance of carbohydrate and fat. These all had to have the packaging removed and be chopped into bite sized pieces, as everything would be deep frozen and negotiated with bulky gloves on. By the time we'd prepared 80 bags, we were thoroughly sick of day-food, but this was a mere taste of things to come.

Drinks were tricky. Pete made the biggest sacrifice of his life (apart from deciding to come to the South Pole to look after me) and agreed not to take any tea. Used tea bags would be heavy items to carry. We took Empact, instant soup, hot chocolate and some particularly yummy instant ginger tea that Rima had given us. I said that he could have all of the ginger tea as I was happy drinking hot water. Harmony reigned.

Much of the food we placed in the not-wanted-on-voyage pile. There was excess of everything. The boxes of noodles looked to be full of chemicals so I chucked them out as well. This was something I would live to regret. Happily, all our unwanted food was sent in the direction of the shanty towns.

The midday deadline was somehow met, although with little sleep. The last item was characterisation of the pulks. I taped two little Tibetan flags to my red cover and also Elsie's Peace Message. She had written (in excellent writing for a baby) "Peace on Earth and goodwill to all grannies." Then I wrote on the sides of the pulk "On behalf of the Earth", "Peace" and "Harmony". Hmm, that's better. We took the loaded pulks and resupply bags downstairs. I couldn't lift our bags as they were so heavy and struggled with one end of the pulks. "Your pulk is the heaviest of all of them," Christian said as he helped me out. I appreciated his considerate nature even though I felt I should be tough and one of the boys. But having such a heavy pulk worried me, as I was all too aware there were just two, not three of us, sharing the pulling. The pulks were placed sardine-like on an open truck and taken to the airport to be put into cold storage for a day. On the way the glorious sun got to work and transformed the nicely cubed cheese and carefully broken up chocolate into artistic globular masses.

Now was the time to relax and enjoy a beer with the boys, at least *they* had beer; I drank water straight from the taps, taking it for granted, not really appreciating what a luxury it would come to be. Everyone was missing their loved ones already. It was certainly a difficult time to be away from families, as it was the week before Christmas. It was nice to hear Gaz talk about his children and see that underneath his highly experienced Royal Marines persona he was a kind-hearted softy. And there were worries, Christian wondered if he would have a job to come back to, it wasn't easy to take two months off during the present banking crisis, for Gary it was his eyesight, as he hadn't been able to have the laser surgery and knew the difficulties he would be facing. Pete and I felt quite close to him as we had been in the Arctic together. We knew him to be courageous.

There was also time for the important business of eating.

Tony had recommended eating two pizzas at once to stretch our stomachs so they could cope with the vast amounts of processing that was about to become necessary. I'm not particularly keen on pizza, but figured it would work equally well with salad and fruit. I devoured plateful after plateful. The hotel had a smorgasbord displaying every type of fresh food possible from this land of plenty with its near-perfect climate. All the racers and film crews similarly went back and forth to the counter for more and more of this wonderful food. The other hotel guests were looking distinctly concerned at this greedy horde that was working its way through the selection of courses. What did we know that they didn't? Was there about to be a tsunami or something?

Yes, in a way. Everything I knew was about to be swept away, wrapped up in the safety of civilisation. The decision to fly out was to be made at 6pm the next day, 18th December. Take-off depended on weather conditions for landing in the Antarctic.

If I hadn't been so keyed up about what the next few weeks would bring, I would've enjoyed everything that we were about to leave behind, like sleeping in beds, taking warm showers, wearing T-shirts, the call of the birds, darkness and twinkling lights, palm trees and luscious tropical plants, the scent of flowers in nature's abundant blooms. But Pete and I needed to buy one last item. Colourful African hustle and bustle and the dance of carnival, raw sights and sounds tried to play with my switched-off senses as we passed enticing street stalls and entered a shopping mall.

We bought an alarm clock. It was going to be important to be awake.

Ilyushin Illusion

The flight was cleared to leave at 23:30. It showed up on the departure board as 82Y9173 – destination: the Antarctic – underneath US604 to London-Heathrow and above KL598 to Amsterdam, just another flight to anyone not about to race to the South Pole. We showed our passports to leave South Africa. There would not be needed to enter the Antarctic, which is unique in the world in that no one owns it. There has never been an indigenous human population; it is now a declared nature reserve and zone of peace dedicated to science.

We were taken by bus past all the other waiting aircraft to an old Russian cargo plane standing alone on the tarmac – the Ilyushin 76. It looked like a huge bird with a long high tail and wings positioned above its belly, pointing downwards, ready to pounce on its prey. This was an adventure plane. The Antarctic company ALCI was running it a handful of times this season from Cape Town to Novolazarevskaya (known as Novo – phew), the Russian research station. It carried scientists and base personnel as well as climbers and adventurers. Racers were a new category.

We clambered up low steps and entered into the bowels of the bird. There were 10 rows of six seats with a central aisle. Behind these were two porta-loos, tied up with anchoring chains like a Christmas parcel to stop them slipping about at inconvenient moments. Further on, past a netting barrier, we could see the pulks and resupply bags. The walls were brightly festooned with enormous flags, which only partly covered up tangles of wires and pipes. There were no windows.

I had been allotted a seat in the back row which afforded a good view of the kerfuffle around me. The racers were wandering around chatting to one another and there was a forest of cameras and sound equipment here there and everywhere, trying to record the palpable air of anticipation. In between were rather serious-faced Russians, no doubt wondering what all the fuss was about. Up the front was a screen – the old type that has to be pulled up and hooked over to show slides. All our in-flight instructions were projected onto this screen, interspersed with the pilot's view from a camera in the nose of the bird. I felt like we were in a theatre and the play was about to begin.

"Please sit down and fasten seat-belts."

Before we knew it, we were watching the plane lift off up over the lights of the city and out across the dark of the ocean. A couple of Russian men in jeans and black polo-necked shirts walked around offering bottles of water, bread rolls and fruit. Ah, the last banana. They also offered us ear plugs, as the engine noise was so great. Rune and Stian, sitting next to me, had to shout through their Viking red beards to be heard, but we were still able to communicate. It felt a bit like sitting next to my sons, as they had the same caring approach; checking that I was okay, updating me on the bits of their lives that were suitable for mothers and not swearing in front of me. I couldn't be certain about this though, for whilst they spoke to me in excellent English, I only knew two words of Norwegian. They had both been soldiers, trained in Arctic warfare and had served in Afghanistan and Iraq. Now they were more settled, living with their respective girlfriends, but preparing for the race had taken over their lives. They had trained hard every day for a year. Whatever the outcome of the race, they were already heroes in Norway.

Some in-flight information came up on the screen:

"Distance from Cape Town to Novo is 4,208 kilometres (2,630 miles).

Speed is 750 kilometres per hour.
Flight time is 6 hours.
Arriving Novo at 03.30 GMT (2 hours behind
Cape Town).
Novo airbase is 505 metres above sea level."

A film was shown, in silence: old David Attenborough
footage about jungle wildlife. Perhaps this was a message to
remember the world we were leaving behind. I would have
preferred to see something about the Antarctic. I longed to
know more about it.

I remembered checking out information on the continent
in my student days. It was the time of life when ideals were
important and practicalities didn't stop the planning of things
(hang on, I hope I'm still in that time). I was fascinated by the
idea of towing icebergs from the Antarctic to Australia. I liked
the image of a 500-million-ton iceberg arriving in Sydney
harbour providing a year's supply of fresh water for that
city of four million. More importantly it could provide fresh
water to grow food on arid but fertile land and help tackle the
problem of feeding the world.

The Antarctic is a third bigger than Europe, nearly twice
the size of Australia and about a tenth of the Earth's land
surface. That's a big chunk of Earth. It's nearly all covered
in ice. This holds 70 percent of the total store of fresh water
in the world. So not only is the Antarctic the world's freezer,
but crucially, the reserve water tank. Next to air, water is the
most precious human resource. We were about to test this.
Humanity needs to look after its water supplies to survive.
The world needs the Antarctic.

We know too that the Antarctic plays a critical role in
regulating the world's climate. The ice reflects back most of
the sun's energy, so more heat is lost than gained. This helps
the excess of heat reaching the tropics, so is crucial in keeping
the balance and preventing the Earth from growing too hot.

These are the days of growing awareness about global
warming (or global *worming* as one observant nine-year-old
described it in her Peace Message). Though many believe the
changes to be part of natural cycles, scientists have irrefutably

stated that humans are speeding up the process of warming. Climate change is a reality. If we don't act, results could be catastrophic. If the Antarctic's ice-sheet were to melt, the sea-level on Earth would rise by about 55 metres. We'd all be visiting London with aqualungs and flippers.

We had seen the Arctic with its minimum summer sea-ice now nearly half what it was 10 years ago. That's rapid melting. That's scary. Poor old polar bear. Unless humans act rapidly, is he to be something beautiful that was here for a while and soon just an item on Attenborough films?

The Antarctic picture is less clear. Whilst the Antarctic peninsula has warmed faster than any other place in the world in the last 50 years, the centre plateau area has been registering colder temperatures. This is believed to be due to the huge hole in the ozone layer above the Antarctic. Now that ozone-depleting sprays have been banned across the world the situation is reverting – hopefully by 2050 to one of a layer of protection against harmful ultra-violet rays. However, scientists estimate that with global warming becoming more dominant, in the next decade a third of the Antarctic's sea-ice will disappear.

Are we hiding our heads in the sand? (That should probably be "in the ice", but it sounds equally uncomfortable.) Is it an illusion that all is well? That the cold hands of humanity can continue on its present course of using up the world's resources in an unsustainable way to satisfy our greed? Are we stuck in the paradox of wanting everything to be perfect how it is and yet needing to change things for the better? Can we find respect for our Earth?

Worries about the Earth's imbalances were whirring around in my mind as I fell into a restless sleep, my head against the vibrating edge of the plane.

Something was calling me in a dream, yet I couldn't find it. I was searching, but I caught the edge of a sense of travelling in the service of the Earth, of bringing healing, of the warm hearts of individuals making a difference. I wanted to hold onto it, but it slipped away, broken by bangs and clatters and rustlings.

I jerked awake and shook my head, attempting to focus on

the information on the screen:

> "Ladies and Gentlemen. We will be landing in
> the Antarctic in 65 minutes. The temperature at
> Novo airbase is minus 10°C. Please change into
> your Antarctic clothing."

Pandemonium mingled with the air of intense excitement.
There was a heap of personal bags between the portaloos
and the seating; finding your own and returning to the
seat was not easy in the bedlam. Even more difficult in the
confined space was removing existing summer clothes and
substituting thermals, fleeces, salopettes and complicated
boots. Then jackets, hats, sunglasses and gloves at the ready.
We sweltered, and hundreds of collective years of dreams
waited.

> "We are passing over the Antarctic Circle at
> latitude 66°33´."

We watched the screen, mesmerised by the carpet of white
spreading out before us – wild, raw, shining forever. As the
huge bird fell from the sky, the runway delineated by green
oil-drums came nearer and nearer. Suddenly, dazzling light
poured through the two little holes that acted as windows
high up near the roof. Ice rushed up to meet the wheels with
a heavy thud. The noise intensified. Juddering, screeching
and swaying now like an old sick elephant, slowly, slowly
we decreased speed. It seemed to take forever to stop but, on
a three-mile runway and beyond, there was no shortage of
forever available.

The opened door flooded the fuselage with light. Then who
should walk in but Father Christmas! Known as Grandfather
Frost in Russia, he had the usual long white beard and red
robes trimmed with white fur, but this figure had rich gold
embroidery too, plus a large crown and a long magic staff in
his hand. This all added to the unreality in my sleep-deprived
mind. Whilst I was waiting for Pete to find belongings
scattered in the fray of changing clothes, a well-fattened
scientist-type sidled up and whispered in a deep monotone
"Grandfazzer Frost has ze power to summon up snowstorms
and blizzards." I thought it best to withhold a reply.

In a daze, I stood at the door and was hit by intensely bright light, a wave of biting cold and a harsh wind. This was how it was going to be. This was the Antarctic. I climbed gingerly down the little slippery ladder onto the ice and nearly fell over. Apart from patches of loose snow it seemed to be rock-hard ice of a clear electric-blue. "Golly," I gasped. "Nobody told us the Antarctic's a skating rink." I glanced up at Pete and we laughed. I knew that underneath his darkened glasses his eyes would be dancing. Never mind the ice. We were here. We were in the greatest wilderness on Earth.

Russian Roulette

Ilooked about me. Although it was the middle of the night, the sun was dazzling, for of course this was the land of continuous light. The air was crystal clear. People were milling around the plane in brightly coloured jackets and hats amidst greetings and hugs and the inevitable filming. Rotund Russians in all-in-one suits were drawing up in skidoos towing long wooden sledges for the luggage. About 300 metres away up a slight incline was a collection of multi-coloured portacabins alongside large red tents amongst pushed-up heaps of snow. This was Novo airbase, our home for a couple of days. In the other three directions my gaze travelled as far as the eye could see to the curvature of the Earth, taking in a sense of nothing that was everything at the same time, a feeling I couldn't quite understand. There were a handful of small snowy peaks on the horizon, otherwise only shades of white ice reaching to the blue of the sky.

Doc Deirdre rushed up with hugs and smiles.

"You can't get rid of us," I teased. I had been concerned in case there was any awkwardness left from our problem times in the Arctic, but the greeting was warm and welcoming. She was, as before, attractive and confident and I felt really pleased that she was along on the race with us. Not too many doctors would have been prepared to do house calls this far away from their practice in the Scottish Hebrides.

"Go and get in that vehicle there," she said, waving at a

shiny dark-blue pick-up truck with huge tyres. "You two are getting special treatment."

I realised that she was taking care of us, as the most vulnerable of the group, in case of cold shock. This is a condition that can come on arriving suddenly in an extremely cold place and can literally put a body into a state of shock. It had happened one year in the Arctic to a competitor who hadn't recovered so had had to take the next plane home. Deirdre told us that even though it was only minus 10°C, the cooling effect of the wind at 13 miles per hour was giving us wind chill of minus 18°C. Anyway, I was feeling woozy and disorientated, so as everyone else was setting off to walk the short distance I felt quite happy that we were getting special treatment. Pete was just pleased to be treated as a respected elder.

The vehicle was one of four, Tony's pride and joy – a specially adapted Toyota Hiluxs, shipped from Iceland. They had been modified by the Icelandic firm Arctic Trucks for the unique Antarctic conditions, in particular to be the cleanest transport available. They had achieved a unique level of fuel efficiency five times more than any existing vehicle here, such as skidoos and caterpillar Hagglers. The plan was for them to transport the race support team, film crews, two doctors and the organisers Tony, Sarah and Kenny, as well as the two Icelandic driver-mechanics Hjalti and Gisli, known as Wolfman. If successful, this would be the first time that 4x4 vehicles had reached the South Pole. Of course in spite of severe tests in the Arctic no-one knew how they would cope with the crevasses, deep snow, gale force winds and intense cold – extreme conditions that make up possibly the most punishing terrain on the planet.

After the race the trucks were to stay in the Antarctic and assist in the bid to have less polluting vehicles. This would make a big difference to the movement of scientists, engineers, personnel and tourists and to some extent obviate the need for the more polluting aeroplane, the DC3, or Basler, which was currently heavily relied upon. We saw two of them parked over to the west of the portacabins.

Novo runway is generally open during the relatively warm, light months of October through to February, except for three weeks at the beginning of January when the ice can soften. It utilises an excellent patch of blue ice which is hard enough for planes to land on with wheels instead of skis, which enables the carrying of heavier loads. Blue ice is formed when snow fallen on a moving glacier has been compacted over time, releasing air bubbles and increasing the size of the ice crystals making it clear. It has then come together in a body like a lake – a good place for spotting meteorites, apparently. Pilots who can land safely on blue ice have remarkable skill (thankfully).

The airbase, nine miles (15 kilometres) from the Russian research station, is the entry point for a vast part of the northeast Antarctic known as Queen Maud Land. This is claimed by Norway, though national claims are rather arbitrary and are on-hold indefinitely. In Queen Maud Land are research bases for Norway itself, South Africa, Japan, Germany, Sweden and Finland. India has one that could be described as "down the road" from Novo – that is, if there were any roads. Most exciting of all is the brand new zero-emission scientific research Belgium station, powered totally by wind turbines and solar panels. It was built with the cooperating know-how of many nations and is a fine example of environmental prioritising. There are 65 research stations spread out across this vast continent, mostly around the seaboard. Hopefully this one is a forerunner of positive changes to come.

It was thrilling to be part of this Antarctic metropolis – or outpost depending on how you look at it – but we needed to focus on what we were doing. Deirdre dropped us outside a large yellow double-skinned mess tent inscribed with ALCI in large lettering. This was where we could gather during our time here, enjoying the mod cons. Warm air was being blown in, there were plastic chairs and green-clothed tables loaded with bottles of relishes and sauces, a clock on GMT which was the time we were going work on, a TV which was great if you liked Russian soap operas, an urn of hot water for drinks and most importantly, a food counter. Here a smiley Russian chef produced surprisingly edible meals for continually hungry racers and explorers. I managed to convey our need for vegetarian meals by various gesticulations such as the universal throat cut sign, though it may have been the appealing-granny-look method that finally clinched it. He responded with fried eggs and fried eggs, the thought of which were to take increasing importance over the weeks to come. I responded by learning, after about the tenth prompting, the Russian word for thank you, "spiceebo". It was good living in the mess tent. What was all the fuss about? The Antarctic was most civilised.

Outside, the mere skin of a tent away, things were different. I stared in awe and apprehension at the void to the south, trying to contemplate what we had taken on. I had a sense that humans were intruding here, that they were not in charge. The land might allow us to cross this wilderness. It might not. Either way the land didn't care. Cold and blizzards would be stalking us. We were about to be involved in a game of Russian roulette.

Of Penguins and Pensioners

Victor, who runs ALCI, had said that we might see Adélie penguins in Novo and that if we did, we should stay still and let them come to us. They are eminently curious little beings, some of the most studied birds in the world as they give a good indicator of changes in the environment. Their populations have been reduced by a third in the last 25 years in line with the warming of the seaboard section of the Antarctic. When the sea-ice declines, so do the Adélies. They live mostly on a diet of krill, the shrimp-like crustaceans which are at the heart of the rich Antarctic food chain. Krill nourish fish, penguins, seals and whales. Their larvae require sea-ice to survive. In some areas krill has declined by 80 percent in the last 25 years.

My friendly Emperor penguins have similarly been affected. Their populations have declined by 50 percent in the last 50 years. Are they a harbinger of the effects of global warming?

No matter how hard I looked, there was not a penguin in sight. But we had to concentrate on the job of putting our tent up, a little way behind the mess tent. Thankfully the area was thick with good snow. It was to be a new experience with the Warrior-designed Nanok tent. Pete and I looked at the flimsy nylon material with concern. It was a tunnel design, small and lightweight which was great, but we wondered, would it stand up to Antarctic gales? Once up, it didn't seem quite so bad, even though the pegs were made of bamboo. Must be okay, Captain Scott had a tepee of bamboo for his tent. We could use skis as pegs too.

The tents were red on the outside, with an inner yellow lining. This meant that when the sun was shining everything inside was a happy orange colour. This would be sure to bring joy and a sense of well-being. We threw in our roll-mats, sleeping bags and personal kit and dived in to enjoy the first taste of our new home. Yes, joy and well-being. For a team of three large lads it would be squashy. For a team of two, one large and one middling (I must insist on being middling even though everyone kept calling me small) who didn't mind brushing up against each other, it was spacious, and loads of room for kit. Ah well, there's got to be a few advantages in not being a three. First job was a hug, important for team bonding.

Rima had suggested that it would be good to try to treat each other as team mates rather than as part of a couple. This way we might have more respect for each other, not get grumpy with relationship issues and be more efficient and quicker with the housework. This would mean less time setting up house at the end of a day and packing up in the morning, which was the ultimate aim so that we could have the most time possible skiing and sleeping. I could see straight away that that wasn't going to work. We knew each other too well. We would carry on just like we usually did, enjoying each other's strengths and frustrated by each other's weaknesses. Like all relationships, times of joy and times of patience. However, pushing ourselves to the limits was going to be a good test of the relationship itself.

We knew our differences. Pete couldn't wait to get the tent up. He loves kit and sorting it, fixing it, having the right tools and gadgets and making sure everything works to perfection. I find the whole kit thing stressful, but I wanted to immediately give a name to the tent and suggested the Polar Bear Cave after Nanook, the polar bear. I thought it gave a nice feeling of somewhere safe to go to sleep, Pete thought it was a stupid name. Pete loves playing with stoves, he's done it all his life and is brilliant at coaxing them when they don't want to sputter. In spite of practice I still found them scary. However, I enjoy sorting the food and making sure everyone's eaten properly. I've done that much of my life as a mother, whilst Pete likes to devour whatever's put in front of him. I love reading and books. My biggest sacrifice ever was about to happen; for the purpose of saving weight I was going to go to the South Pole without a book (unless I just snuck one in). Pete, as a man of action, would rather be doing something.

We have different types of minds, he will remember that something happened at 2:10pm, whilst I will not remember what day it is, but rather how it felt (though these days as pensioners we often both struggle to remember that something existed at all). He will always win at chess and I will always win at Scrabble, no matter how many times we play. He is a natural leader, I am a natural follower, although he complains that when we dance I don't follow him but go off and do my own thing. Generally we make a good partnership and balance each other out. Now, with just the two of us, communication would be easier and we could relax with each other and be ourselves, but even if the rules of our relationship changed, one thing would be certain; we were both determined to reach the South Pole under our own steam. We were dreaming the same dream.

There was one tiny fluffy cloud scurrying along in an empty blue sky as we started organising our skis. Apparently there had been five days of whiteout and snow just before we arrived, producing five year's worth of snow. That's the Antarctic. Unpredictable. We were lucky to miss that. The Antarctic is technically a desert, most of the central plateau area receiving less than a handful of millimetres of snow in a year, but here on the edge of the continent things could get quite Christmassy. Novo is only 47 miles (75 kilometres) from the ocean, or rather from the sea-ice.

Shiny new cross-country skis were issued. Pete's were 200cm and mine 180cm, so not unlike the length we used 10 years ago for downhill skiing. I was pleased that they were wider than the ones I'd had in Norway. These were black and grey with a picture of a face that covered the tips of both skis.

"Who's that?" I asked the Warrior.

"That's Fridtjof Nansen," he replied, looking mortally offended that I didn't know.

Luckily, I had an inkling that Nansen was a famous Norwegian explorer who had won the Nobel Peace Prize, so the Warrior continued to speak to me, but later while he wasn't looking I cut pieces of duct tape, stuck them over the face and with a felt-tip pen wrote "Harmony" on one ski and "Peace on Earth" on the other. I knew the power of the mind. At home I have positive affirmations and sayings around the house to absorb, it helps counteract the negativity of things like watching the news on TV. I would be looking at those skis day after day, I needed something inspirational to me.

We had to fix skins underneath the middle part of the skis. Skins prevent the skis slipping backwards when going uphill and would help over lumpy ice. They used to be of seal skin but now are synthetic. We glued them on and drilled holes to secure them with wires. That was the skis sorted then, or was it? We noticed that Christian was also fixing on an extra heel binding, it was a wire loop. "It'll give you more stability," he said. "The Norwegians aren't bothering and only have the three-prong toe bindings. They're hardcore." We listened to Christian. He had cross-county skied for Britain. We went for the heel wires. It was worth the extra time clipping into the skis to get some stability.

We toodled around on the skis. Where there was ice it was more like being a big-foot clown putting on a ridiculous show, but thankfully okay on snow. I also practiced towing my pulk. I decided to name it Khandro. (It's important to name things. Think how differently one might behave to one called Flower compared to one called Dogpoo). Khandro is Tibetan for "sky dancer", giving a sense of ease and lightness, just what I needed. I have no idea why Pete named his Henry.

We enjoyed chatting with the other teams who appeared to be in good spirits too, though I felt that QinetiQ, the youngest and strongest Brits, were finding it hard having the pressure of being the British favourites to win the race. James and

Ben had taken part in a race rowing across the Atlantic three years earlier. James, as a twice Olympic gold medallist, was a winner at heart. Ben was in fact recovering from a nasty bout of a flesh-eating bug known as *Leishmaniasis* involving chemotherapy, which finished only one week before leaving. Made of stern stuff these Brits. Whether they liked it or not, they had a reputation to uphold.

Like most of us, they were inexperienced in the polar environment and were struggling to sort out gear and sew all the many things that needed to be adapted for the extremes of what we were about to face. Like gaudy-coloured tags on zips so that they would be operational with big gloves.

Stian and Rune of team Missing Link were wandering around in reindeer jerkins looking cool and relaxed, as though a race to the South Pole was an everyday occurrence. Was the outcome a certainty? By no means. In this environment anything can happen. Even pensioners can win (joke), and something like one tiny piece of equipment not functioning can change the whole outcome.

James was having trouble with his new boots. He cut the ends off them, leaving a gaping hole of sock. It wasn't that his super-fit body was too hot. No, he was running out of solutions for finding enough toe space. The Warrior came to the rescue with bits of tent bag and glue producing a fashionable new look. I felt sorry for QinetiQ having to be in the public eye. Their every move was being recorded on the cameras, every thought on the sound systems. It must have been quite an intrusion, adding much stress, but they were great at being dashing and informative and sharing their world with adoring fans. It was good to know that we were going through something extraordinary, in a far away land that most would never be able to see and that millions of people would go through it with us too.

Their film crew got on with everybody well. Alexis was on camera along with Keith; Roly and Georg on sound, but they were each able to take over the other jobs when necessary. They were with TwoFour, one of the UK's leading production companies. In spite of their long experience, this was surely the most logistically challenging documentary series ever thought up.

Like the rest of us they were concentrating on eating everything possible. We weren't the only ones. There was a lone skua bird hanging about outside the mess tent working on the serious feeding ground of scraps. He was a bit like a large brown gull with beady eyes, black webbed feet and a wide bill with a hook on the end. I had always associated skuas with eating penguin eggs and chicks so I didn't feel very warm towards him. If he had been a penguin I would have been ecstatic. Bad luck being born a skua and not a penguin. I didn't know I was so prejudiced.

Maybe it's because I love penguins. I'm sure everyone does who's seen the film *March of the Penguins*, which tells the amazing life story of the Emperor. How they march, in a long waddling line, with great devotion up to 70 miles across the ice, away from the sea where they are at ease swimming and feeding on fish, to find a safe breeding ground. How the parents take it in turns to guard first the egg and then the chick, safe and warm in a tummy flap above their feet, and then they huddle together through the coldest winters on Earth.

I had been having doubts about the extra weight of my Emperor, Gaius, not that I was going to admit that to Pete. But I tied a bootlace around him as a harness and attached him to the front of my pulk. He fitted there well. Yeah, of course he must come. A penguin-powered pulk would give all these macho teams something to think about. No contest. Presumably the other teams were too busy preparing gear to have the time to visibly quake at the sight, but Petter, from the Norwegian TV crew, came by our tent to capture him on film.

"Why've you called him Gaius?" he asked.

"It's because we're racing on behalf of the Earth and Gaius is the male version of Gaia the Earth, so he carries that spirit. Also it just so happens to be the name of a wise wizard who knows all the answers to everything, which is really useful, but maybe that's the same spirit as the Earth anyway."

Petter nodded. He was an earnest lad, revelling in the experience of being here. He was also an expert polar traveller and, I felt, would love to have been one of the racers. His tall production partner Martin, on the other hand, had no experience in this environment. In fact he'd never even camped before. Nothing like throwing yourself in at the deep end. Good for him, I thought. Life can pass by if it's not grabbed whilst presenting itself.

I've always liked the "soul growth" principal. That souls have the opportunity to be here on Earth to experience the play of life. That various scenarios will enable the soul to dig deep and find positive attributes, such as compassion or patience, so producing a stronger, more loving soul. Thus raising the consciousness and vibration of humanity and the Earth. Under this theory one can sit and wait for challenges to grow with, which could be illnesses or various negative dramas, or one can go out and create challenges that are positive and exciting but give the same result of soul growth. I've always tried for the latter, looking for what makes me feel really excited and going for it, then life falls into place with more ease anyway. That's the theory. *Carpe diem* – seize the day. Though with the current speed of life it really needs to be *carpe punctum temporis* – seize the moment. Hylton came by and confirmed this by saying, "It's not the things you do in life that you regret, it's the things you don't."

I knew how precious this opportunity was and how incredibly lucky we were. As we settled down for our first night in the Antarctic, with my headband covering my eyes to block out the light, we were rocked by the flapping sound of the wind playing with the tent. I felt like we'd been here for days already. My nerves had evaporated and there was a deep sense of fulfilment.

I woke up sweating and hot. Hot? How could I be hot? This is the Antarctic. It was a reminder to develop a sensitivity about temperature. Sweating is dangerous. It over-cools the body. Our sleeping bags had been designed to operate down to minus 45°C, which meant that a balmy minus 10°C needed alternative arrangements, such as sleeping underneath, rather than in, them.

It was a clear day with a cold wind which eased as the

day developed and high cloud started to build. Around midday the southerly wind from the Pole dropped and the temperature rose. Briefly, the wind blew from the direction of the sea. It was as though the land was breathing, touching something vital and alive. Harshness and beauty, darkness and light, suffering and compassion – so vast that the mind of man couldn't encompass it.

But there were still jobs to do. Like cutting our tent poles down in size to make them easier to fit into the nylon sleeves and attaching stronger guy-lines. Plus our GPSs had to be programmed with coordinates, and we needed to chuck out everything we could to lighten our loads, including considerable amounts of food. I wasn't planning to chuck out cheese, though, it was rather precious, but somebody else thought so too. I left a large bag outside the tent and came back later to find the ripped up remains with telltale beak marks on. Skuas went down in my estimation even more. We had lots of nuts though and they were very heavy. I dropped a large bag for Gary at his tent and then the same for Phil. It was a good thing I didn't know then how much I would regret this later.

"Please don't give Phil more food," said Rachel, despairing at the weight that their team, Due South, were pulling as well. She had been on a North Pole race before with Hylton who was a lovable bear of a man. Together with Phil, being so knowledgeable and strong, their team should do well.

On the way back to our tent I saw Mark, the blind explorer. "Are you alright, Mark?" I asked.

"I can't find my pulk," he called back.

I went over to help. His pulk was barely half a metre from him, but he wasn't bothered. He was relaxed and organised, he was used to coping in tough environments. Since he had lost his eyesight he had competed in an amazing array of marathons, iron-mans and medal chasers that would have been more than impressive for any sighted person. It was lovely to see Simon, a muscle-bound rugby coach, helping him around in such a patient, caring way. The Warrior was joining them to help in the race itself. Their team, South Pole

Flag, had already won all the medals in my book.

All that was left to do was the final food sorting. It was then that I discovered I'd done something really stupid. I'd left lying around the tent two bags of nuts. They'd all been eaten – two weeks' supply of nuts. Only this time it wasn't skua's beak marks, but pensioner's. There was nothing I could do about it now.

All the teams were taken to the Russian base for a quick tourist visit. We travelled across icy wastes in the slowest, bumpiest machine on Earth, a caterpillar Haggler, which felt like being enclosed in a police van drawn by something like a small tank. It descended to 120 metres above sea level in an area known as the Schimacher Oasis, which was so much warmer that there were rocks around. In fact it felt like being on the moon, but more desolate. The base was a collection of lonely pre-fab buildings. I searched for signs of life, but saw nothing – not even lichen or the largest land animal, the wingless midge who comes with his own glycerol anti-freeze system. The thought of wintering over here during the six dark months with temperatures down to minus 70°C didn't bear thinking about. You'd need lots of glycerol.

The following morning was 21st December. At home it was the shortest day; here I was in the longest day on Earth. At the Pole the six months of daylight would be broken by the sun disappearing below the horizon on 21st March. I woke up, nervous, with a nauseous stomach and dry mouth. It was time to leave Novo and set out on the acclimatisation trek. We wandered down to the runway and watched the Ilyushin take off. The awe-inspiring giant bird gathered speed, trailing a cloud of snow and flew up into a heavy mackerel sky. Passengers had come in from various bases and been joined by those from climbing expeditions. They were leaving the continent to return home. The next flight out would be on 30th January. That would be us, on our way home, but for now our journey was just beginning.

There was still not a penguin in sight. Good thing we'd brought our own.

March of the People

This may be the Antarctic, but we still had 1,400 miles to go to reach the South Pole. We were told that from now on everyone should work in metric distances. Oh help, that was tough on the old brain. Multiply by eight and divide by five. That made it 2,240 kilometres to go – the distance from London to North Africa.

We were given position coordinates. The acclimatisation trek was to be from Novo at latitude 70° south to a camp at 72° south, following longitude 11° east – a distance of about 160 kilometres. The plan was then to be picked up by a plane and transported to the start of the race at 83° south, from where we would race the last seven degrees, still following due south along this longitude, to end up at the South Pole at 90° south. Simple – but then plans often are.

The main purpose of the acclimatisation trek was one of altitude preparation. Most of the Antarctic continent is a high plateau, due to thousands of years of layering down of snow compacted into glacial ice. The weight of this is so large that if all the ice were to melt, scientists predict that the suppressed Earth's crust would rise by 1,000 metres (wow!). The elevation at the South Pole is 2,835 metres (9,306ft) of which it is estimated that 2,700 metres is ice. That means that the ice underneath the South Pole is not far short of two miles thick (double wow!).

For the race we would be on the high plateau at this

altitude of nearly 3,000 metres. However, the barometric pressure here is 30 percent lower than expected for this elevation, due to less weight of overlying air because of the Earth's rotation. This makes the oxygen molecules disperse more widely, which effectively makes the air feel thinner, a process exacerbated by cold. Therefore, the physiological altitude is the equivalent of up to 4,000 metres. This is a bit like hanging about just below the top of the Matterhorn, in the Alps (something which I have done too often on attempts to reach the summit).

Being at altitude affects human bodies. Altitude sickness is not much fun. It manifests as headaches, fatigue, shortness of breath, nausea, lack of appetite and light-headedness. It is often worsened by vigorous exercise. When severe, it can lead to high-altitude cerebral oedema and pulmonary oedema, either of which can be fatal. It is hard to predict who or when it will strike. Pete and I knew the consequences of not being able to cope with altitude all too well after suffering severe altitude sickness on our peace climb on Chimborazo. It is possible for bodies to physiologically adapt to coping with the effects of altitude by gradually increasing elevation over a period of a couple of weeks. This gives time to produce a higher count of red-blood corpuscles to utilise oxygen more efficiently. So moving slowly from the altitude of 505 metres at Novo over a period of 10 days up to the camp at 72° south at 2,357 metres would effectively give us the altitude acclimatisation that we needed.

Along the way we would be getting used to the cold and how the whole process of living in this extreme environment works within shouting distance of the expertise of the Warrior. He would be able to offer hints, not only on how to navigate, but how to survive.

The most beneficial tip on survival seemed to be to stay out of crevasses. When the Antarctic ice-sheet moves towards the sea as all glacial material ultimately must, it reaches a steeper descent at the edge of the plateau. Here, along with meeting other obstacles such as mountains or pressure ridges, or going over bumps in the bedrock far below, the ice cracks produce deep fissures, usually in clumps that can go down several hundred metres – the friendly crevasses. Our acclimatisation trek through mountainous areas was to be full of crevasses. Once on the plateau, the risk would be diminished. Until that time, the Warrior was to guide us up through this heavily crevassed area. The race organisers had concluded that it would be a better race if the competitors actually got to the start-line alive.

The crevasses might have been easier to spot from a birds-eye view. The great white open landscape was snaked by mountain ranges – some covered in snow and some exposed rock – through which wide rivers of ice were creeping at the pace of history, cracking and splitting while responding to the forces of nature. Then the folds of the rivers of ice would have been seen, and perhaps, looking closer, a long line of dots threading their way, uphill against the current, meandering around the folds and following one after another. Long skis on their feet, sticks in their hands, trudging, left foot, right stick... right foot, left stick... each dragging belongings behind, shelter, fuel and food – people on the march.

Like so much in life, the bigger picture makes sense of things, but from my narrower perspective on the ground I found that crevasses were really hard to detect. This was because they were generally covered in snow and to an untrained eye it was possible to stand on top of one on a 15-metre-wide snow bridge – in a whole minefield of snow bridges – and not even know. The Warrior asked us to follow in his tracks and when appropriate, pass messages down the line. So when we stopped and I was told, "there's a few crevasses to the left, see," I turned and repeated the message to Pete and then studied the expanse of white. All I saw was more expanse of white. Was that a line through the snow? Imperceptibly, a shadow, or was it my imagination? I had thought that they would be more obvious. Pete nodded wisely and added "Only small ones, of course," in a disappointed voice, which didn't do much for my confidence. At least one of us found crevasses interesting.

In spite of the crevasses, it was great to finally be on the move. I'm sure all the racers felt the same. All the months of preparation were now being put to use. I enjoyed the group energy of similar purpose. Teams Missing Link and QinetiQ were under pressure as the Norway vs England game had been stirred up by the media. No doubt competitive beasts would be unleashed, but outwardly there was little competition between the teams, apart from the inevitable good-natured banter like, "I'll wait for you at the Pole." There was an undercurrent of everyone wanting to help everyone else. An unwritten agreement that the only thing that mattered was that everybody got there safely. Perhaps Homo sapiens, when stripped of civilisation and faced with survival, isn't that different from the Emperor penguin.

Our marching line was led by the Warrior with two long poles about three metres in length, attached to the end of his pulk. The other ends of these were attached to Mark's sticks so that he could feel the poles with his hands and sense every bump and configuration approaching under his skis. Simon followed in front of me. At a slight bend I turned and, like looking out of a train window, saw the rest of the long waddling line strung out behind me. It wasn't easy to stay balanced on the move whilst twisting my head, but I glimpsed figures marching steadily onwards, followed by the red covers of their bulging pulks. It was easy to identify the teams because their outer windproof jackets were colour coded. Danske Bank was grey, QinetiQ sky blue, Missing Link royal blue, South Pole Flag midnight blue and Due South mustard.

Only Southern Lights was different. Pete had gold, but my original small-sized gold jacket had had too tight a hood and the only alternative had been a purplish-pink described as magenta haze. Obviously, the universe wanted me to wear magenta. For fun before leaving I had looked up the meaning of the colour "magenta" on the Internet. It was described as fast and exciting, associated with the self-realisation of true strengths in order to give to others. It was akin to the violet used for "keeping-going" in the White Eagle healing system. I couldn't have wished for a more perfect colour. It was vibrant

Training - out on the pull along the South Downs Way. Tess takes the strain, whilst Pete takes a rest.

Training Norwegian style. Tess swimming with skis on, in the middle of a frozen lake.

Tess playing with granddaughter Elsie.
The reason for the quest was to help protect
the Earth for future generations.

March of the people. All the teams together on the acclimatisation trek,
before the race.

Lining up for the start of the South Pole Race.
Rachel, Tess, Pete, Stian, Rune, Ben and Ed.

They wove their way up through Antarctica's beautiful mountains.

Would Tess and Peter ever reach the South Pole? Would they ever see the famous barber's pole surrounded by its twelve Antarctic Treaty Nation flags, blowing proud in the harsh wind?

Pete: Tess' knight-in-shining-armour.

Finding a way through sastrugi fields that resemble pods of dolphins.

Pete on snow melt duty in the tent.

Tibetan flag flies at camp Southern Lights, whilst Gaius the penguin stands guard on the front of the pulk.

The camp at minus fifty degrees Centigrade, with shifting snow drifts.

Place of peace for a crystal ceremony in the pure white wilderness.

and feminine and I felt like myself in it (one can't walk to the South Pole in just any old colour). Gold was described as a powerful spiritual colour, but its most frequently quoted physical association was that of the expression of a noble man. Seeing Pete striding along behind my pulk looking tall and dignified in his goggles and face mask, I could have told them that anyway.

I soon changed from sunglasses to the complete cover-up system of goggles and face mask, as my nose was feeling sunburnt already. We were wary that this was the most ozone-depleted place on the planet. Only some of the others had covered up their faces. I had noticed that Pete and I tended to wear more layers of clothes than the others. Perhaps old bodies find it harder to keep warm. I was also somewhat fearful of the cold. It was hard to find the right balance of what to wear. I was trying out the gaiters and my feet were much too hot, but apart from my right foot rubbing and a few niggles in the ankles, my body felt pretty good. I felt happy with the motion on the skis. At this stage we were going slowly enough for style to make little difference.

The pace gave me time to keep looking at the far curve of the horizon, broken only by tops of mountains here and there poking through the ocean of snow like floating icebergs, and to remind myself, almost in disbelief, that we were here. Also that it was such an honour, a privilege, to be heading into this cold white wilderness. My sense of being an intruder had fled. I felt humbled and that, as long as we showed respect, we were welcomed by Antarctica and its shining lights. I didn't feel overwhelmed, rather more the start of a growing feeling that I was part of this land and that this was where I was meant to be.

As soon as we stopped to make camp there was no more time to be lost in my own thoughts. We had to go into immediate action. Pete and I fell into a quick routine that was to serve us well. I had learnt years ago to let Pete choose the spot for a tent. Not that it was very difficult here, with thousands of square miles of flat space, but the wind moulds the ice to its own artistically-lumpy specifications. He liked to do that bit. We had pieces of ribbon (pink because I had bought the ribbon) tied to our ski-sticks so we could see which way the wind was blowing. The direction that the tent was pitched was vital. It was designed so that the rear of the tent had to be directly into the wind. That way the wind would flow over the tent rather than try and blow it over. He placed his stick where the rear of the tent should go. In the meantime, I unstrapped the tent from his pulk. Together we tipped out the tent from its bag, making sure neither blew away. The rear end loop and those either side were secured with bamboo pegs. Then the three tent poles – which were already half in their sleeves – were shunted in completely, and awkwardly fixed at the ends. That's awkward with warm hands and thin gloves, but swearingly annoying with numb hands and thick gloves.

Then we split jobs. Pete anchored the guy-lines with skis and bamboo pegs, setting the tent to his perfection. After this he grabbed a shovel and, with superhero energy at the end of a hard day, dug up snow to put all round the valances. The theory of this is to prevent the tent and everything in it from blowing away. A useful theory. In the meantime, I dragged the pulks to the front door and chucked in roll-mats, sleeping bags, food bag, personal bags, stove bag, day-sacks and anything else that needed to come in. Then I filled up the two big plastic bags with snow, dived in and made order out of chaos, just in time for Pete to come in, too, and there we had it – a five-star polar bear cave.

That first night of the march we were still developing our slick technique. Pete was establishing his routine with the stoves. I was establishing my routine with the food. We were getting used to how to dry gear on the overhead hanging net and the system to melt enough snow for the huge amounts of water we needed, but that wasn't what started the argument, compounded by the difference in our natures:

"Pass me my socks bag."

"Which one is that?"

"It's the one that's labelled socks."

"But what colour is it?"

"I don't know. It's labelled."

"But all your bags are the same colour. Why haven't you got different colour bags for different gear? We haven't got time to try and read tiny labels."

"***!"

Wars may have been started for less futile reasons.

I went to sleep irritated and upset. We were in this unique and stunningly beautiful wilderness, and we were arguing over the colour of our bags.

On awakening, the sun was warming up one side of the tent which seemed to filter through to our hearts too. We were both making an effort. I resolved to find what I could change within myself to make a difference to our relationship. It wasn't until we were packed up, on skis, pulks attached and in line on the march that I had time to think about it. The temperature was an icy minus 15°C. In a few days our bodies would became more tolerant to the cold and this harshness would feel relatively mild.

Was it as simple as that? If I could be more tolerant then what I had previously perceived as harshness would feel relatively mild. Maybe it was. If I react to upsets and become angry and judgemental then my blood pressure rises, my vibration drops and I suffer and feel dreadful. Whereas if I am tolerant and loving, then I recover quickly, my vibration rises and I feel great. It's really nothing to do with what's coming at me, it's to do with myself. Like the Dalai Lama says, it's to do with my own inner peace.

Giving, I knew, was the magic ingredient. I turned and gave Pete the sign of crossed ski-sticks in the air which we had agreed between us meant "love you" and sent a bubble of loving energy towards him. I was rewarded with a return sign of crossed ski-sticks. Great. My knight-in-shining-armour was back on his steed in my thoughts. The universe had given me an opportunity for soul growth. All was well with my world.

It was slightly confusing that the Warrior, leading the line, was also communicating using ski-sticks. This avoided motorway type pile-ups when people were skiing too close to the pulk in front. The sign of two ski-sticks in the air seemed to be for "stopping in 10 minutes" and the sign of crossed ski-sticks for "stopping now", or maybe he was just a very loving person.

We were heading up a gradual incline on flat easy-going snow, with distant peaks of the Drygalski mountains shimmering in two directions, when he signalled a stop. "Lunchbreak," he shouted. This happened every two hours. Psychologically, it felt good to have lots of lunchbreaks. Somehow the words snack break or tea break didn't have the same sort of yummy anticipation. We all turned our pulks away from the wind, so we could sit on them and munch with our backs to the gale. It always felt like there was a gale within a couple of minutes of stopping, because our body temperatures plummeted so quickly when they were stationary.

The Warrior was excited. He pointed to a group of peaks far over to the west, dark quartz-syanite rocks standing proud like cathedrals above the white of the snow, bravely withstanding the winds of time. "They're Fenriskjeften, the Jaws of Fenris. To my mind they're the most beautiful mountains in the world. The highest is Ulvetanna, the famous Wolf Fang which was first climbed by Norwegians in 1994, using portaledges."

I knew about portaledges, the hanging ledge system like a stretcher attached by slings to a point in the rock. I'd hung in one for 11 days during the Earth Summit in Rio in 1992 doing a protest climb on the Sugar Loaf mountain face. It had been difficult then in a warm climate, but to wait out storms on a mountain face thousands of feet in the air, in mind-blowingly cold temperatures, trying to melt snow for drinks, would be seriously challenging. These Norwegians were tough, for sure.

The Warrior enjoyed these mountains too because of his philosophical outlook. The Fenris was the monstrous wolf of Norse mythology. Tales equate him to the force of nature. The gods, being fearful of him, tried to tie him up. Attempts with various increasingly strong chains failed. Eventually they succeeded with a golden chain made of the magic ingredients of roots of mountains, women's beard, bird's spittle, the breath of fish and the sound of cat's paws. The story has the meaning that the real strength of life comes not from "That which is", but from "That which is not" – unquantifiable attributes such as love, positive attitude, faith and hope.

It is said that Fenris is destined to eat the whole world at the end of time, amid great battles, but after the destruction a new Earth will arise, green and fair and all will live in peace and harmony. Some ancient cultures predict the end of time as 2012. Even if it's only the end of time as we know it, or it's a very gradual change, one thing is for sure, there will be change. That is the nature of life. All things are impermanent. As individuals we can affect the direction of change, not only by what we do, but by how we are, what we hold in our hearts. If we can hold warmth then the new Earth can be one of peace and harmony. Perhaps we'd better get on with things.

That day we marched for eight hours and covered 20 kilometres, which was fairly typical of the next few days. The idea was to go at a steady slow pace so everyone could build up confidence and fitness. I was conscious that a group must always go at the pace of the slowest person and there was no doubt that I was the slowest. It was always going to be like that. I hoped the youngsters weren't feeling too frustrated. Around 3pm I was feeling very tired and time seemed to be dragging.

"C'mon," the Warrior said to me not unkindly after checking I was okay. "I want you out in front. See those three mountains on the horizon. Aim for the middle one and lead a straight course." Suddenly I was in a situation where everybody else depended on me. I had to concentrate hard on where I was going and not make a wiggly line, which I didn't find easy. I was the individual making the difference. It woke me up. My whole attitude altered which changed the way my body moved from snail-like into go-for-it mode, and I found myself full of energy. Funny thing, this energy game. It's not straight-forward. It can change in a second at the whim of the mind.

I was to learn that, as long as the mind is strong and in control, all is well, but when the body is depleted and moves into exhaustion mode, the mind can do strange things. Fear can invade and turn it into a battleground.

Gathering of Fear

Christmas came and went and with it the weather armistice. It was back to work with the wind. It woke me in the night, just a flapping and a moaning – enough to know that there would be no more balmy times. An icy blast greeted us as we started skiing, our faces well protected. Climbing steadily, we read on the GPS that our altitude was now over 2,000 metres, effectively 2,700 metres. Pete was coughing a bit, but overall we felt that we were doing well with the acclimatisation. I was enjoying the movement of the skiing and pleased to be keeping up with the pace.

When my next turn came to practice navigation by leading the group I tried using the wind method. Because of the openness of the plateau, the wind is generally expected to be consistent, so the idea was to note the direction of the pink ribbon streaming out from my ski-stick and try to maintain a course to keep it at the same angle. However, even with the flattest snow there are variations with every step and I was soon going wiggly. To see something in the distance helps. Previously I'd had a mountain to aim for. Now we were leaving the mountains behind and all that lay ahead was a vast expanse of icy waste. Literally nothing but snow lay before my eyes.

The fairly flat snow was great for skiing on, but not for finding your way in. The Warrior pushed me to find little bumps that looked different and to concentrate on those.

Cold Hands, Warm Heart

There was a little dolphin-shaped bump here that looked slightly lighter, and a little dolphin-shaped bump there that was just catching the light. Yes, on looking closer, there were actually a few dolphins about, but I found it really hard to concentrate on them and hold a straight course. As soon as I took my eye off one to see where I was putting my skis, I would lose it and end up leading the line off course. Everyone else seemed to have managed well. It was frustrating to be so bad. I wished there were a lot more dolphins about.

This is not a sensible thing to wish for. Towards the end of the day the incline eased and we came out onto a plateau which had a totally different surface. It was all hard wind-carved ice, sastrugi – in fact a whole sea of dolphins. It was rough and horrible, like trying to walk across a badly ploughed field against the ruts while towing a dead body. My skis kept crossing and I fell over. This not only dented my pride, but I found it was a real struggle to heave myself upright again. It did make me feel slightly better when I saw the big and the strong, both James and Pete, fall over too. Oh help, I thought, if the whole of the plateau's going to be like this, I'd rather go home.

"You can opt out here if you want and go back to Novo. Are you going to do the race or not?" Tony asked bluntly as he called us out of our tent a couple of hours later. He and the Warrior were going round to speak to each of the teams. We were close to the spot where the plane would pick us up and take us to the start-line. Just another eight kilometres to do tomorrow. Meanwhile, Tony and his team would drive the vehicles overland.

"It's minus 23 here at the moment, plus wind chill. At the start-line it's minus 35. Add on wind chill. That's down to minus 40 something. Seriously cold. The support crew setting up the start-line camp have been having a tough time. It's no picnic." He looked me straight in the eye. It was intimidating. I felt like I was in trouble at school. I knew that he knew that I was the weakest of everybody. That made me the biggest liability.

I didn't dare look at Pete. He would see my doubts. "Yeah,

we're up for it," I said, not very confidently.

"Yes, of course we are," Pete reiterated. At least *he* sounded certain.

Apart from my loss of composure on the sastrugi field I had actually been feeling good about things. Now that all disappeared and I recognised the worry-worm sneaking its way into my mind, bringing in the fear. I was not actually quite sure what I was fearful of. It was something deep-down, almost primeval.

It got worse in the night as a gale gathered strength, feeding the fear. A terrifying roar ensued, and the tent shook violently. The snow slashed against the outside. It seemed a miracle it was still standing when the Warrior came round in the morning and shouted low against the tent, "We're staying put today."

"What? Can't hear."

"We – are – not – moving."

Thank goodness for that. Time to catch up on some sleep. I snuggled deeper into my sleeping bag, but I couldn't nod off. It was good for the body to have a rest, but bad for the nerves. The shaking fear and all the din was making it hard for me to think straight. I felt all tied up in a knot of dread and anxiety. I tried to calm myself by going through my meditating routine, knowing it was my way of turning inwards for the strength I needed. There's a spiral in my mind where I go through four areas; cleansing, affirmations, contemplation and healing. It was during the third that I sensed a voice inside, quiet and Goddess-like:

"Do not be afraid... no harm will come. This is just a test."

A soft strength of universal love filled me and I felt more relaxed. Wriggling out of the bag, I went through the lengthy process of dressing to go outside. Unzipping the inner tent, I made sure I crouched in the tiny porch area to close that one before opening the outer one, stepping out and quickly turning to close it up. There never seemed to be an occasion when the zips didn't get caught in the material. It was just one of those things trying our patience to the limits, and then they would break as though designed to do so, so that by coming apart easily they could also come together with no harm done. Maybe it was a Warrior principal.

Today was no exception. I had to jiggle the large tags up and down until they worked. The storm hit me ferociously and I swayed with it, trying to hold my balance. I could barely make out the other tents through the whiteout. They seemed such a long way away. I staggered around tightening the guy-lines. Then dug into the snow to get at my pulk which was placed with Pete's on its side at the windward end to give us some protection. Poor Gaius was most indignant at his precarious position, lying on his side. I ignored him. After all, penguins were designed for this weather. I found the spare food that we needed and struggled round to the front of the tent to thankfully get back inside.

I was just removing the snow, or "degombling" as it's known, when Pete came out with, "Without this tent we're dead. Albeit the material hasn't ripped, the guy-lines have held."

He wasn't concerned. He was just trying to say how good he thought the tent was, but a pang of fear gripped me as though something was trying to smother the thinking processes in my head. I waited for a lull in the sound of hissing snow to reply, trying really hard to be clear and positive. "Maybe this storm's a good thing. The delay might mean that the dates will be right for the peace ceremony."

He shrugged. "Well, we can't do anything about it. Let's enjoy a day in the tent."

We settled down to some sewing. There seemed a lot to mend or adapt. Pete started with his salopettes straps. I patched the holes in my felt boot liners, a regular job, but we soon became cold. Even with all the vents tight shut there seemed to be an icy breeze blowing through. What a difference it made without the sun. There was nothing to warm us. They say that a human body creates the equivalent warmth to one 100-watt light bulb. Well, two bulbs against the might of the Antarctic didn't seem to go far. We decided to light the stoves, mindful that we were on limited fuel. We usually melted the snow on two stoves in the little end porch and then brought one of the stoves in to the inner tent afterwards. Now we used both inside, careful to remove the boiling water before steam enveloped. It was precarious moving around the tent, but how lovely that precious warmth was. We ate the bean curry packets (favourite) and the chocolate mousse puds (revolting). Then, whilst the stoves were on we enjoyed a sponge wash in an inch of water. We felt good until noticing the plastic pouring jug was too close to the flame and had melted to a distinctly smaller version.

Converting snow to water is a long and essential process. With two stoves lit, the large and middle-sized pans had to be filled with snow from the snow bag by scooping with the small pan. Some starter water was important too so that the pans didn't burn. The snow melted slowly down to a quarter of its volume and needed to be topped up frequently. Then when boiling, it was poured into flasks and bottles.

When all the bottles were full, we turned the stoves off and snuggled back into sleeping bags. Time to write my dairy and return to my own thoughts. The storm was still relentlessly raging. It was good to feel close to Pete. I looked at him lying on his back with his earphones on grooving to music (Queen, no doubt). "I'm having fun!" he shouted. Yes, he looked completely happy. I felt so pleased that we were together and lucky to be supported by his rock-like strength at a time when I felt so wobbly with fear. All the annoying day-to-day things were suddenly not so important, and I felt a deep overwhelming love for him.

I wondered if at some level I'd chosen to experience this, to push myself mentally and physically to try to find that place of purity and calm in the midst of the storm. I knew at this moment I was in touch with a greater universal strength. I felt like I was touching both joy and terror at the same time. Does adversity make it easier to touch a Divine joy whilst in a terrifying situation? The roar of the wind became stronger. I could swear even the sleeping bag was rocking with the shaking of the tent, but I was helped by positive sensations jumping into my mind, as though fighting the growling wind: a force of loving strength from the crystals, and a memory of the film crew asking me why I was here. "It's for my little Elsie", I had replied, "for her generation. To make a difference, to help make sure that there is a beautiful world for them." Perhaps we have all chosen to be here and prepared over eons of time to help the ascension of the Earth.

The merciless blizzard howled unabated and I slept in peace.

"Tent down at 10am," came the order. It was minus 29°C and still the gale raged. We prepared and went outside, but the wind was too strong and there were new orders, "Tent down at midday." We waited in the tent and found tasks to busy ourselves with. I was trying to sort out a system that suited me for attaching my Matty-mitts gloves. No problem to put on and off when warm but a nightmare in the wind with numb hands. I was considering the possibility of a long cord round my neck, or clips to a karabiner on my jacket, or ties to the jacket sleeves.

"I'll try wrist loops," I said. So Pete took the scissors and cut one of our precious spare bootlaces.

"Look what you've done. You've cut them twice as small as needed," I said crossly, overreacting. "There's no room for error here. We have to get everything right. It's the only way we'll survive." He didn't say anything.

An hour later whilst I was starting to pack my pulk, barely able to see through the swirling snow, I tripped over a guy-line with two roll-mats in my arms. One of them slipped from my grasp and sailed away on the wind, not even touching the ground. Drat! I rushed after it, floundering in deep drifts. I was no match for something flying. How could I be? Puffing and panting I stopped to catch my breath and held on tightly to the other mat. I turned back, annoyed with myself. How stupid. It was a serious loss. The floor mats gave us not only cushioning, but more importantly an essential barrier from the cold. There had been two wrapped in the one that had gone. Luckily we had enough left to spread, but thinly. It would mean gaps and damp sleeping bags. How quickly had my own hasty words come back to haunt me, "There's no room for error here. We have to get everything right."

Determined not to let my guard down again, I packed my pulk and we managed to strike the tent without anything else blowing away. I took extra care with the bag for the bamboo pegs and the tent-bag itself. It was made of tough material. Tonight we might try using that as floor covering.

Within minutes of setting off, all as close together as possible in the whiteout, I saw one of the dark blurry figures ahead crumple and collapse. It was Mark. Many hands picked him up and we waited while he recovered. He bravely insisted that he was okay and that he'd only passed out because of some pills he was taking. He continued with a strong arm to lean on either side. It was a reminder of how vulnerable he was out here, of how vulnerable we all were out here. At least we didn't have far to go today, though the conditions made up for that. With wind chill we were down to minus 40°C and my hands were numb for what seemed like an hour after the stop even with shaking and punching to try and return the circulation. The horrendous sastrugi was still there to taunt us. Most of the others were struggling too over the lumps and bumps, skis out of control, continually fighting it. Phil and Rachel took their skis off and figured that in today's conditions walking was 10 times more energy efficient. I asked the Warrior about it.

"Oh, it's a good idea to take your skis off in difficult stuff," he said, "but this is easy." And he continued floating along as though out for a Sunday stroll. Norwegian hard core. I wondered if there was any truth in the rumour that he'd been brought up by a Viking elkhound.

We made camp at 72° south, happy that the acclimatisation leg was over. It had been not far short of 160 kilometres (100 miles). So far, so good. Most of the height up onto the plateau had been made. We were one step closer to the Pole. To the South Pole and beyond, yeah! I celebrated by hydrating with one of the three herb tea bags that I'd brought and Pete had Rima's ginger tea. We thought of her. She would have loved this, but we were doing okay as a pair. Now all we had to do was climb on the plane and we'd soon be at 83° south for the start of the race. There was only one small problem. Although the wind had eased somewhat, we were in the middle of a whiteout.

No plane could possibly land in this.

I had it in my mind that any delay would be positive for team Southern Lights. That there would be much less distance to race and it would increase the chances of being at the South Pole for the 29th January.

I was wrong.

New Year Messages

The following morning, visibility was just as bad. Although we could hear team Due South to one side and team QinetiQ to the other, we could barely see their tents. It was 30th December. The day the race was meant to start. We could do nothing but wait for good weather, not only here, but at Novo so the plane could take off and also land near the start-line. This was a lot to ask of Antarctica.

There was more sewing to do, but sitting in the tent was becoming frustrating when our bodies were so geared up for motion. Besides, my granny knees were cold and achy with their old trick of seizing up if still for too long. So when conditions lifted, it was any excuse to go out and play. I needed to fix a gaping hole in the outer layer of my pulk. I had no idea how it had come about. I whooshed out all the snow that seemed to pile in however careful I was and tipped it upside-down. The Warrior showed me how to make a flat covering of glue over the hole that I hoped would dry in spite of the lack of sun. Then I watched Rachel carving a lovely snow horse. It looked like a Tibetan wind-horse which traditionally carries the messages from prayer flags and it set me thinking that as we were going to be hanging about we could do a Peace Message reading.

In view of the recent winds we decided to build a good wall at the windward end of our tent. We were just about to start when I saw James building a huge wall at the end of theirs, displaying large amounts of youthful energy.

"Hey James," I shouted. "Would you like to build one for us as well? We could pay you a bag of day-food, chocolate and stuff." I'm sure he would have helped anyway, but at the mention of the word "food" he was with us barely before I had finished speaking. In no time at all we had a great wall behind our tent and everyone was happy. Maybe, I mused, there are better trading commodities than money in our world. I could just see the Channel 4 TV newsreader telling us, "Today's index is up by 3,000 bags of chocolate."

We were, in fact, all coming to the end of our food stocks. Tony had to drive back from half way to the start-line with one set of the resupply bags. The next day, New Year's Eve, he gathered us together for a briefing in the shelter of his vehicle as a penetrating wind loaded with ice bullets was rising.

"Novo's buried in snow. They can't dig out the planes." There were shuffling signs of discontent as he continued. "Forecast is not good. There's only a 30 percent chance of a plane landing here, whereas if we move 14 kilometres south to a position with greater visual contrast we should have a 100 percent chance. We'll move tomorrow and prepare a new landing strip." Ah, new orders. At least there would be some action. In the meantime, there was action to undertake of a less military kind.

The Peace Message reading was in a draughty green mess-tent. There were a couple of folding chairs, food boxes and camera cases to perch on which gave a false impression of warmth. We sat bundled up in duvet jackets, gloves and hats whilst the blizzard gathered strength outside, plummeting the temperatures. Undoing Empie, I pulled out the prayer flags and attached them to the central pillar. They fluttered, yellow, green, red, white and blue, looking a little forlorn as gusts of icy air raced through, a tiny offering of sacredness in this vast great wilderness.

After recording the scene on camera, Keith was keen to be part of the ceremony. He describes himself as a shambling Cambrian, I would add "huggable". In fact, he and all the film crew seemed to have a special warm-hearted quality here in this incredibly tough filming location, the coldest place on Earth.

"So how do the Messages make a difference?" he asked.

"Well, that can be seen in many ways," I replied. "I think that the actual conceiving and writing of them makes a change in that person, reaching to a deeper level than they might have otherwise. For example, a child making a pledge to bicycle to school with the intention of saving carbon dioxide emissions is bringing in respect for the Earth, and of course the fact that the Message is to be taken with great effort and spoken at the South Pole means that it is something important and not to be forgotten."

"So speaking them out is like the Tibetan tradition of flying prayer flags to send out blessings? In other words, like oral prayer flags?"

"Exactly. And the Tibetan word for blessing, Chinlap, means the transformation through energy. So I see it like the blessings helping to bring about transformation of the mind for the better, for the raising of consciousness."

"Beautiful."

Pete and I were also joined on and off by Simon, Mark, Petter, Roly, Georg, Hylton and Alexis, so we were represented by the nationalities of Wales, Ireland, Norway, Austria, South Africa and England, a little cluster of humanity. I handed out the sheets of Messages and in clockwise turn we spoke out a Peace Message each. For nearly three hours we voiced the 1,300 pledges, wishes, prayers and hopes that had been sent from caring hearts. They were touchingly beautiful. Expressing love and concern for our Earth, her systems, her animals and her peoples, a coming together of the energy of peace and of light. There was no shortage of wind-horses to take them away galloping in the face of the storm, leaving our handful of tents, isolated (bar scientific bases and a few explorers) by a whole continent of ice, far out onto the winds of the planet.

We were deeply cold to the core, but happy that in these last hours of 2008 we had honoured our Earth.

Cold Hands, Warm Heart

On leaving the mess tent the plan was to return just before midnight for a shared joke and a drink to see in the New Year, but conditions were reaching a wild intensity outside and I had my doubts that we would want to battle our way back later. It was only 10 metres or so to our tent, but we had to drag our resupply bags and this became a struggle through the snowdrifts that had appeared. Weirdly, it seemed like they were almost alive. There was shifting snow everywhere. The Antarctic was on the move. We gratefully reached our tent and battened down.

The two little porch areas have no ground covering, but are usually sane places with at least some feeling of insideness. The front one served as main door, storage for day-sacks, duvet jackets and a shovel, refilling of fuel bottles, emergency deep-hole loo when conditions were unbearable, and general degombling of snow. It was an area the size of a triangular doormat. The other end porch served as the kitchen. We kept the filled plastic snow bags here and the stoves bag, along with spare fuel bottles. Here was the space to lay out two of the stove boards which Pete had imaginatively designed to hold securely both stove and fuel bottle.

It was important to remember that although there was a full doormat size here too, the roof tapered to the top of the main inner tent. This meant that any shooting flame – which was an essential part of lighting the stoves – was at risk of burning the tent down. Today that was not our main worry. We were greeted by the sight of the end porch, and everything in it, covered with an extra layer of snow. Somehow it was coming through the lower end of the zip. Hurriedly, Pete brought a stove into the inner tent and lit it. Usually it's noisy. Now the wind was even louder. We savoured the warmth as we prepared water for Mediterranean vegetable pasta meals, poured the boiling water into the bags waited a long five minutes, stirred and wolfed it down along with a hot chocolate. My thoughts were not on the food, but on that hurricane howling which seemed to penetrate every line of defence in my body. Turning off the fuel, I watched as the flame continued for a minute, spluttered and died.

Pete took off his salopettes, pulled out his sleeping bag and wriggled in for warmth. I wasn't so sure. Maybe I should stay dressed and be ready to go out. We'd been through storms before. Somehow this one was different. There was the deafening roar and the violent shaking of the tent, but now we also had heavy shifting snow. We could all be buried. Sitting and waiting in the tent had invited the fear in. It was well and truly back. A deep creeping fear, seeping through my being.

A voice outside shouted against the gale, slowly stressing each word. I strained to hear.

"New – Year – cancelled. – Too – dangerous."

"Thanks," I shouted back, but doubted it could be heard.

That wasn't the only thing I doubted. How could we manage if there's this sort of weather on the race? How would we cope if there's a problem, just the two of us with no one else for miles around? All the support would be thrown into chaos. Tony wants to show all those people that say it can't be done, that they're wrong. He wants to show them that he can do it. Waiting in this violently-shaking stormbound tent, I wasn't so sure who would be showing who.

I realised I was shaking too.

I pushed back all the layers of clothing on my wrist to reach my explorer watch, hard and comfortingly solid.

The time. Look at the time. It's one minute to midnight.

60 seconds to go... fleeting like the 60 years of my life, now asked to fulfil its destiny.

I held my breath, as though this would make time stand still, but the inexorable changing of the seconds continues as though trying to keep up with the pounding blood in my veins.

60 – 59 – 58...

If it weren't for the deafening roar of the wind trying to blow the tent to oblivion, I would hear it. Instead I feel it like a throbbing drum.

Fear.

57 – 56 – 55...

The sides of the tent now hold a cold deathly hue, standing between us and the battering blizzard. I can't tell if the violent shaking is from the power of the storm wind or from the soaking deluge of spindrift snow crashing angrily against this obstruction in its path.

Relentless.

54 – 53 – 52...

I prepare in my mind for the possibility of a sudden rip, a gape instantly inviting in the elements, of intense cold becoming wild ice cold. Of grabbing my boots and orange and maroon gaiters, my magenta jacket, layers of pink and red gloves, dark green goggles, strewn amongst the heaps of multicoloured gear. How quickly it would all be buried and turned to white.

51 – 50 – 49...

Beside me, Pete's fallen asleep. Should I wake him? My eyes search his face for any sign of concern. No, it's peaceful and relaxed. I know that without such a racket going on I'd be able to hear him snoring, his breath rhythmically at work. The sound would have been comforting.

48 – 47 – 46...

What was it that he'd said just a little while ago?

"Scary isn't it, not knowing if the tent will hold?"

I had looked at him then, unsure. He's not meant to say things like that. He's my knight-in-shining-armour, his mere presence affirming, "I shall fix everything. I am big and strong for you and will always protect you." Knights-in-shining-armour aren't meant to say things like, "it's scary, isn't it?".

45 – 44 – 43...

His mouth twitches in its own dream. So this moment is mine alone. I'm the one to carry us consciously through the gateway of this New Year, this new beginning.

42 – 41 – 40...

I picture Plumtree Cottage, far away in England, soft gentle brown tones, the sort of home that hugs you warm and safe, oh so safe. No harm could ever come there. I see a family New Year scene, writing letting-go messages onto bits of paper and burning them in the welcoming log fire. Marking this special time by walking up to the top of the hill to make resolutions and stare up at the stars feeling small and insignificant, yet part of something wonderful. I miss the dark. It enables stars to be seen and the little candle in the window shining out hope for the new world.

39 – 38 – 37…

I will not forget to make a resolution now.

36 – 35 – 34…

Hang on, Father Time, hang on please. Wait for me.

33 – 32 – 31…

Shivering.

I would rather be sitting at home in the warmth with a purring pussycat beside me, asking nothing more than to be loved.

30 – 29 – 28…

So you won't wait. I have to be here now in spite of your hurry.

27 – 26 – 25…

I am trying not to think of Captain Scott's words written in his diary nearly 100 years ago, "Dear God, this is an awful place." He was waiting as we are, waiting for the storm to pass. Yet he waited too long.

24 – 23 – 22…

We cannot wait. We have unfinished business to attend to, this time we will do it, this time we will not fail.

21 – 20 – 19…

And what of the race? Why is it important to get there first? What if the winner makes it but nobody else does? Because there's no shelter, no food, no fuel for water.

What if, in the world, "those that have" make it, but nobody else does? What if there are no forests, no fertile soil to grow potatoes in, or no chickens to lay eggs. What then?

18 – 17 – 16…

What on Earth are we racing for?

15 – 14 – 13…

We're racing *for* the Earth. That's what.

But the anxiety running up and down in my blood merges

with a primeval foreboding, that of the continued existence of mankind.

12 – 11...

I cannot see whether my survival is a microcosm of the greater physical survival, but what is clear is the vision of this mission. The mission is so huge, so important at the greater level, it has to be done whatever the personal cost.

10 – 9...

Though why am I needed to do it? Why me, when there are so many big strong explorers? Why pick on a little old granny when there are so many youngsters just itching for action?

8 – 7...

I hear a boom that adds to the sound of roaring, of howling, whether from the wind banking or the shifting snow, I don't know, but the air passing through the tent now tastes of washed clean sorbet.

6 – 5...

I pull my hat down low over my ears, the thick wool rough on my fingers. Well, it's too late to question. I have to do it.

4...

And yet...

I feel deep within, the touching of a long gone memory of a pack of animals baying, of the hunter becoming the hunted. Basic instinct calming the terror. There is only one thing of importance.

3...

I am here now.

2...

My New Year's resolution is simple.

1...

Involuntarily, my hand clenches into a cold fist, fighting to let go of fear, compelled by instinct born of thousands of years sculpturing the cells of the human body.

I WILL SURVIVE!

Waiting Game

Unlike many New Year resolutions, this one seemed to have worked – at least until 6am. In the dull grey light of the following morning, I could see that snow was trying to entomb us. On both sides of the tent a wall of white had accumulated between the inner and outer layers of the tent. From time to time in the night I had bashed my side ineffectively to try and keep it from hardening. I poked my head out to view 2009, and was hit by a blast of driving spindrift. At least the wind had died down a little, but snow had eaten everything. Drifts half a metre high were not only pushing into the tent, but had completely covered the pulks, the sticks and the shovel. The wall that James had built us had been brilliant and protective, but he, Ben and Ed had had to go outside every two hours throughout the night and dig out their own tent. It seems that they had enthusiastically built a wall so high for themselves that it had gone beyond a certain point which had then caused the reverse effect, bringing snow pouring into the lee gap engulfing the tent itself. Too much chocolate, no doubt.

Tent down at 2pm was the news. It took us an hour and a half to dig out everything and pack up. James and Ben generously helped us do the tent. I really appreciated it. Because of the altitude or maybe just all the sitting around, I was feeling breathless, light-headed and cold. On top of that my knees ached and my goggles had misted up. I hastily rubbed the insides with my glove so as to be able to have some visibility before they froze, but there wasn't much to see anyway. It was whiteout blizzard as usual. My main concern was that I was pulling a huge weight. Since unloading the resupply bag I had our 15 days of food in my pulk. As Pete hadn't yet loaded up with the fuel, he took his day-food packs which helped, but skiing became a nightmare challenge.

I was determined not to be slow. Having sat around for days, everyone seemed to want to go at flat-out speed without stopping. Within 25 minutes I was hot – too hot – sweating and panting hard. So much of life here seemed to be on the wrong ends of the temperature scale. I just needed a minute to undo the under-arm zips on my jacket, which always made a big difference, but I didn't dare stop as I knew I'd never catch up. I looked forward to the race when we could go at our own pace and stop when we felt like it. Something seemed to be back to front there.

Thankfully it turned out to be only a couple of hours to the new campsite and, at last, here the weather seemed to be clear. It was back to wall-to-wall horizon. The vehicles had bashed up and down with heavy weights in tow and made a new runway with a cache of fuel drums, green in the sea of white. Now all we needed was a plane. The word was that maybe tomorrow one would come for half of us and then return the next day for the second group. Maybe.

Having been sweating, my temperature plummeted as soon as we arrived. By the time we had the tent up and I'd filled the snow-bags, I couldn't feel my hands. Pete was finishing off outside by building a wind-protected loo-wall and I started on the stoves. My numb fingers decided that lighting matches was impossible. Knight-in-shining-armour to the rescue and warmth soon returned, but it was a lesson in what not to do. Working fingers to start stoves could mean survival.

Warmth in the tent also returned with the arrival of the sun. What a joy to experience it again. We relaxed over a meal of vegetable tikka, though the insides of my lips were still sore from sunburn, even without the sun. Strong stuff, the ozone-free radiation here. Pete enjoyed having new supplies and worked his way through bags of sweets and chocolate. Even knights-in-shining-armour must be little boys sometimes.

The sun made me feel positive. I knew that it was up to me to cope with my fears, by changing my thoughts. Simple. Right. The temperature had risen to only minus 18°C with a gentle wind chill. But I wondered, no doubt like everyone else, that if the conditions were so good, then why hasn't the plane arrived? The waiting game seemed to be continuing endlessly. There was an air of restlessness around. The important thing was to keep busy. There was always sewing. I cut up a neck gaiter to make double inners for my Norwegian mitts and put clips on my Matty mitts to attach them to my jacket. Then I sewed tags onto our big Tibetan flag, tied it to a ski-stick and planted it outside our tent.

I was reminded of all the Tibetan children trying to escape over the snowy and cold Himalayas with sparse clothing and food in search of an education. I was glad we were fundraising for schools so that some of them didn't have to make that journey. Pete also flew his "Everyone Active" banner for his leisure centre. We then did a test walk with the compass rig that he had cleverly designed. It attached to waist and neck and enabled a hands-free view of the global compass. After allowing for the deviation from magnetic south, the compass checked out brilliantly against the GPS reading. This meant that we could navigate following the compass without having to use the GPS which uses huge amounts of batteries in the cold.

What else would pass the time? Well, there was visiting tents and chatting. Our visit from Ben prompted an incredulous outburst:

"Wow! You two are amazing."

What was it? We knew we were looking cool wearing all the up-to-date gear...

"Your tent is the only one that doesn't stink of smelly feet."

Well, there are standards to keep up.

We visited Christian, Gaz and Gary and chatted (keeping just a little distance away). They were ensconced on huge blow-up mattresses that looked really comfortable. That was doing it in style. We hoped that there might be an opportunity to travel together for a little bit of the race. It wasn't a very sensible thought, for of course they were looking forward to following their own strategy but a nice friendly thought just the same. We needed to remind ourselves that this was a race. We weren't too bothered about strategy and knew we would probably come last, but there were other priorities.

We watched as Tony drove off with the vehicles to head for the race route. Then I set off for a little walk by myself. It felt good to be without skis and a pulk. I headed straight for the sun with the wind behind me. I felt warm and excited to be completely by myself. The snow reflected the sunlight in huge plates as though someone had taken a knife and smoothed the icing-like surface. It was as flat as anything we'd experienced so far. After half an hour I stopped and turned and turned and turned. I could just make out the few dots of the tents on one horizon. Apart from that, for 360° there was only snow and sky and a discernable line where the two met and I was here in the middle of it. There was a profound sense of purity and light. I breathed deeply to drink in the magic, feeling the power and the peace, and yes – the aliveness of it all, but I felt vulnerable. I saw the fragility of man allowed to settle in this ice kingdom for a few seconds. I understood the smallness and the vastness. I headed back to the dots. This way was very different. I was going into the wind. Now the cold tried to freeze the skin on my face and I had to keep wriggling my nose to keep the blood moving and concentrate on protecting it. I knew to never let my guard down, but I had forgotten.

Nearing camp I saw Mark and Simon out for a run, doing press-ups every few metres, no mean achievement at this altitude of 2,400 metres, effectively 3,200 metres. I admired their strength and fitness. Only slightly less energetic was the game of frisbee, followed by cricket. Pete joined the boys and I watched from the relative warmth of our tent, quite mesmerised. Not so much by boys playing cricket with a shovel and snowballs, riveting as it was, but by the sight of total grandeur that filled the sky behind them. There was a huge blazing sun around which hung a rainbow solar halo, formed by ice crystals suspended in the air when conditions are cold and clear. It was complete with two bright spots on either side known as parhelia or sundogs. I didn't tell the Warrior, but I knew it was a good sign.

We went to sleep rocked by the sound of the flutter of the Tibetan flag guiding us on our journey.

I was brushing the breath-ice off my sleeping bag when the Warrior came round the next day.

"Chance of two planes arriving at 2pm. Be ready."

"Yeah! To the South Pole and beyond!"

All systems go. We rushed around preparing and packing up. Snow out of pulk and everything else in, including Gaius. It wasn't a good time to discover that our emergency shelter somehow had been wrecked and didn't look easy to mend. Then, at first imperceptibly, then gradually louder, the sound of a drone reached our ears. Everyone stopped what they were doing and watched as underneath the high sheets of cirrus cloud a dot appeared, then it had wings and finally a tiny twin-propeller plane, blue on the top and red underneath, circled overhead. It banked away, turned and with skids fixed precariously beneath the wheels, bumped down on the snow in a great blaze of white streaming out behind, coming to a shuddering halt near our tents. Taxi anyone?

Within 10 minutes another plane had appeared.

I had a lump in my throat. At last...

Ten of us managed to squash into one plane. Whilst piling high some of our pulks alongside the little rows of seats and strapping them with a webbing net, I chatted with Jim, the pilot.

"I'm from Saskatchewan. Sure thing... we fly down every season from Canada. Good old birds, these Baslers. They're converted DC-3s. Go forever, they do."

It was a good thing that we didn't know that after

dropping us off this plane was going to crash. If we knew everything that was going to happen, we might never get out of bed and where would that leave our soul growth in its lovely play of life? It's the changes of experience that weave our rich tapestry of consciousness.

That morning I'd been feeling scared and vulnerable. Hugs with Pete had helped; also remembering the parting advice of Jan from the White Eagle Lodge. She had suggested visualising a six-pointed star of light for protection, letting it flow down like a tent around me and the others to hold the energy strong. She had said that by undertaking our journey with the intention of bringing peace and light, we were doing it for everyone and everything and that it was a way of grounding spirit. I had thought about the difference between body and spirit. I knew that as spirit I always endure and am strong, but as body I take on fear and anxiety. Yet there is an overlapping. I had resolved to try harder to hold myself strong in spirit.

I had thought of the Southern Lights, whose name we carry. Research has shown that they occur simultaneously with the Northern Lights. When the Aurora is visible in the north, but not visible in the summer sky in the Antarctic because the sun is shining, that doesn't mean that they are not here. Just because something is not visible to the human eye doesn't mean that it is not here.

And I'd heard that Goddess voice again saying:

"All is well. All is very well."

Now on the plane I was feeling excited and confident about the race. I knew we could do it.

We munched our packs of day food, knowing that it would mean one bit less weight to pull. I didn't find mine very exciting. All I really wanted to eat was the nuts and cheese, but food is warmth. It was so cold on the plane. My feet were like ice-blocks. Today I had tried the blue socks on top of the inner felt liners, but because they were so tight I think they restricted the air circulation. Sometimes less is more. Apparently there was heat up the front of the plane, but some of us had to be in the back. At least we could wander about a little between the pulks, though it was hard to talk as it was so noisy. We could see open sky through gaps around the door (which appeared to be tied on with a strap) and for added excitement visit the coldest loo in the sky, a bucket in a cupboard, but the view out of the window made up for everything. We were flying low at only 2,500 feet. It felt like we could almost reach out and touch this great shining silver ball that we were skimming across. It was just possible to make out striations of sastrugi waves. Apart from that all was smooth, all was peaceful. Above us a giant sun hung dazzling in a clear blue sky.

After a flight of six hours and 1,200 kilometres we came down bumping and jolting into deep sugary snow. We were met at the plane door with a big hug from Sarah who was running the communications.

"Go and put tents up over there." She waved us over to a racers area nicely marked out with wooden pegs as though space was restricted.

I stopped to put on my duvet jacket. After the cold of the plane I felt deeply chilled. Not unlike a vintage car, my old body always took a while to get started and warmed up. In fact it was only minus 22°C with small wind chill. Because of all the delays we had missed the minus 35°C temperatures and huge wind chill that they'd been experiencing here. That was a good thing.

It didn't take long to check out our new location. We were a little collection of green and red tents and two vehicles. The support team were Kenny as organiser, Sarah, Wolfman and Doc Ian. Then there were the two film crews and the six racing teams, all in a vast empty white wilderness about as far away from anywhere that you could reach on the planet. This was the start-line of the race at 83° south, 20° east, at an altitude of 2,400 metres. We were 756 kilometres from the South Pole.

Sarah came to our tent to give us details. There were three sets of coordinates to go through, and then the halfway checkpoint. The race was to start at 10am tomorrow, 4th January. We had to be at the South Pole by midday on 28th

January at the latest. That left 24 days less the compulsory 24-hour checkpoint stop. So, 23 racing days. This meant that with no spare time for any hold-ups, we had to cover a minimum of 33 kilometres a day.

Pete and I looked at each other with a desperate gaze. We had signed up to enter the South Pole Race after we had been told at the Newbury launch that we would have to cover a minimum of 15 kilometres a day. At the kit meet in Oxfordshire Tony had confirmed that the slowest could do 25 kilometres a day, although we had honed our training to the distance of 28 kilometres which had been given in a previous email as the minimum. Now, just as the race was about to begin, we were being told that it had to be 33 kilometres.

Circumstances change for sure. The logistics of the whole thing were astronomically complicated, dependent as they were on extreme weather conditions. We had just experienced what could happen. It was amazing that the race had actually reached this point anyway, but that didn't help us. As I was the weakest and the slowest, it would be team Southern Lights that was most affected by these changes. We both knew the implications. If we couldn't keep up, we would be picked up by the vehicles. That was the one thing above all else that we didn't want. We had to face that we could only do our utmost, but for the first time an element of doubt crept in.

Pete raised his eyebrows at me in question. I replied with a shake of the head. My mind was churning and I could see that his was, too.

There was absolutely nothing we could do about it.

Go!

A buzz of excitement surrounded the camp. The race was on. After days, weeks, months and even years of preparation, this was it. We were about to go. Everyone was rushing about here and there, calculating and discussing distances, filling up fuel bottles and sorting food – 13 days' supply to keep us going, with spare, until the checkpoint.

Even though there had been little competitive talk up until now, suddenly the air was full of good-natured bantering. Rune and Stian set up their Norwegian flag, red with a blue cross outlined in white, and called for everyone to listen:

"Look at this flag. The next time you see it will be at the South Pole."

Pete joined in. He held up our Tibetan flag, twice the size of the Norwegian one, and shouted back, "You wanna get yourselves a decent flag." He then tied it to a couple of ski-sticks and proudly placed it outside our tent where it unfurled and blew out in the breeze. It spoke to me of the purpose of our peace mission. Not for the first time I wondered why a flag was so emotive. I could understand why they used to be carried into battle. Here we were on the eve of a great contest and it was the flags that were stirring the heart towards victory.

Inevitably, it was Norway versus Britain that the fun was about. Would Amundsen's win over Scott be avenged? I surprised myself by being caught up in it and saying to

James, Ben and Ed, "Make sure you do it for Britain!"

But I knew that all I really cared about was that everyone stayed safe.

Pete had often joked about pensioners winning, but I knew we were reluctant racers, not bothered about beating anyone. However, this didn't mean that we weren't intending to go all out to reach the South Pole in the allotted time. To this end we recognised that it was important to not over-push ourselves at the start as there was a long way to go and our bodies could crash out and ruin everything. Our plan had been to be quick and efficient with the tent routine, keep the overall goal in mind and to begin sure and steady with 10-hour skiing days. Then, to gradually build up the time on skis.

This was to be possible using a roll-over method whereby we used days longer than 24 hours, so that there was less tent-time in a day. Alternatively if we were finding the time on skis too long then we would find a rhythm of eight hours skiing, four hours in the tent, eight hours skiing, eight hours in the tent. Both of these methods were possible because of the 24 hours of daylight. In any case, we would go into overdrive nearing first the checkpoint and, finally, the South Pole knowing that the end was in sight. The fact that the goalposts had been moved with the shortening of the time didn't really fit in with our plan. All we could do was take it one step at a time.

Amongst the hectic preparations we settled down for six hours sleep. I felt strong and good. In the morning after our usual quick wake-up hug I asked Pete how he was feeling.

"Yeah, really excited."

"Aren't you nervous at all?"

"No. I feel completely secure. Albeit I've been wondering how I'll cope with the altitude, and also my goggles misting up."

I was feeling nervous and scared. Nothing new there. I felt so sick I couldn't eat breakfast.

"Why're you nervous?" both camera crews asked in turn as we were packing our pulks.

"I don't really know" I replied shrugging. "I guess it's all so... so big, so imposing."

But the sun was shining and it was a beautiful day with little wind. The temperature was only minus 25°C. We had been told that the weather would be more stable up here on the plateau nearer the centre of the continent. Let's hope so.

Sarah asked everyone to take it in turns to visit the vehicle to view their emails on her lap-top. It seemed totally incongruous. In just a few quick minutes, pages of precious messages from family and friends appeared on the screen as well as some extra Peace Messages. I came away with a wonderful sense of all the people thinking about us at the other end of the world, of being loved and cared about. In particular I remembered "See the Light, feel the Light, be the Light", a good mantra. How amazing it was to receive them. What would Captain Scott have made of these communications? It's hard to imagine today, but in 1912 it had taken a full year for the world to even hear about the tragedy of his death.

And would Scott have hugged Amundsen, given the opportunity, as warmly as all the competitors now did? "Go well. Stay safe. Good luck" from every individual to every other one. It was more like a family party. All except the Warrior who was striding up and down having transformed from guide to competitor, still looking like a prize warrior.

"Line up! Line up!"

As we gathered together in the last minutes, I was agitated. The word was that two of the coordinates weren't necessary to go through. Apparently there had been a worry about crevasses, but we should not now be concerned. Also the coordinates for the checkpoint had changed. I wasn't sure I had them down right. Nothing like setting off across the Antarctic not knowing where you're going. At least we shouldn't be able to miss the South Pole. They couldn't change those coordinates.

As Tony was still on the way here with the other two support vehicles it was Kenny, an Arctic military Special Forces operator, who stood in front of us. It reminded me of the start of the North Pole race and of my desperation then.

161

Now I lifted my head in a moment of pride. I thought of the long journey that Pete and I had taken over the last two and a half years since then, of the huge effort and focus that we had needed to reach this point, of the months of trying to find the money and another team member, of all the endless, hard training, of Pete's medical problems and operations, of the struggles against all the odds. And we were here.

"We are at an historic moment, the start of the Amundsen Omega3 South Pole Race," Kenny declared. He didn't need to shout. There was little wind and no other sound that could possibly interrupt. "This is the first race to the South Pole since Scott and Amundsen nearly 100 years ago. Do not forget we are in the middle of the coldest, the windiest, the highest and the most remote continent on the planet, nor ever forget Antarctica's unforgiving nature. Go well, go safe."

We lined up facing south, 14 men and two women (and one penguin) with hopes and dreams flying high, in front of a rope that had been laid out between the two vehicles. Oh help, I noticed that the binding on my left ski wasn't done up properly and was about to come off. As I was fixing it, the count-down started:

"10 – 9 – 8..."

"To the South Pole and beyond!" I shouted with my stick in the air.

"Please no further," insisted Rachel, to my right. "It'll be quite far enough."

"3 – 2 – 1..."

The horn from one of the vehicles blared – and was drowned out by cheering.

Go!

We were off.

Sixteen pairs of skis went over the rope followed by 16 pulks in a surge of eagerness and excitement. It was as though a wound-up spring had finally been released after all those days of going slowly and of waiting. All the promises of not going out too hard or too fast were forgotten. As had the heaviness of the loaded pulks. Never mind about being careful not to sweat. The South Pole Race set off, as Gary pointed out later, like a bat out o' hell.

The positions quickly settled down into line much as predicted. Stian and Rune took the lead for Missing Link, with James, Ben and Ed of QinetiQ in hot pursuit. Then came the Warrior, Simon and Mark for South Pole Flag, closely followed by Rachel, Phil and Hilton for Due South. Christian, Gaz and Gary of Danske Bank were a little way behind and finally, the plodding pensioners Pete and Tess for Southern Lights.

Pete fell in behind me. We had discussed that it was best if I led so that he couldn't rush off and leave me a long way behind. Also, I was better at turning my head to check behind without having to stop, which makes one surprisingly off balance. This was something that was tricky with jacket hoods up, but I usually wore my wind-proof hat so could manage for longer without a hood. No need for hoods once we warmed up today. It was perfect conditions, though it wasn't long before the straggly bits of my exposed hair became encrusted with long dangly bits of ice in the "winter princess" look, as the Warrior called it.

All my nervousness dissipated as soon as we started skiing. Certainly, I needn't have worried about the navigation. The other five teams were leaving us a highway route of ski tracks. With Danske Bank not far in front, I tried to settle into the good pace that we had been used to on the acclimatisation leg. The snow was heavier and more granular and the sastrugi wind whipped into larger dolphins, but the going was no problem. How lovely it was to have the feeling of tiptoeing across a vast ocean of snow. Already I had that familiar sense that here was nothing, but also everything. It was so beautiful. Then came a shout from behind:

"Tess!"

I stopped and turned around. Pete was a little way behind. I waited for him to come alongside.

"What's the matter?"

"I feel exhausted."

I stared in disbelief. What? "But we've only been going an hour."

"I'm sorry. I need to rest. I've got no energy at all."

He sat on my pulk, which was the designated resting seat for us both as it was the one without the tent. I grabbed Pete's day-food and water bottle; his body must be running out of fuel, surely. We had been pretty hectic before setting off, without a lot of sleep and going off fast. Yet somehow that didn't fit together. Normally that wouldn't have made any difference at all.

"I feel so shattered and can't catch my breath. It must be the altitude."

"C'mon we've got to keep going or we'll get cold." After 10 minutes we were already chilled.

We set off again at a slower pace. With a heavy heart I watched the little black figures of the other teams become dots and disappear over the horizon. We were now on our own. There was just us and nothing but white snow 360° to the horizon.

Pete plodded bravely on and I tried to coax him to eat and drink at every opportunity, particularly chocolate which is usually wonderful with its feel-good factor as an energy boost, but he seemed listless. He also started complaining about things, which is normally quite out of character.

"It's alright for you. You're not pulling twice as much weight as everyone else like I am. I've got all the fuel and the tent and the rope..."

He went on about the rope so much that I suggested we swop pulks. Pulling his pulk, I realised that his was actually lighter than mine, because mine had the full complement of food in it. After we swopped back he didn't mention pulks again, but he was saying strange things.

"I'm not going to push myself when I'm exhausted, or I'll do some damage." That wasn't him. This race was billed as the toughest endurance race in the world. We had both entered knowing full well that we'd frequently be pushing ourselves beyond exhaustion.

After the next stop I attached his pulk to the end of mine. It's not something I would've normally done lightly, it's the sort of thing that is possible because you know you're doing it for someone else. I surprised myself by being able to pull two pulks for about half an hour, albeit slowly. When he took his back, the break seemed to have done some good.

We crept on through the day until 7pm when we stopped and put up the tent. Our daily schedule call-in with the satellite phone was from 7:30 – 7:40. I had set my watch alarm for 7:20. It was crucial to remember this timing. If any team didn't call in, a search party would be alerted immediately. I had been designated the phone person. This meant that I had to keep the battery warm in my thermal pocket against my body at all times. Then the warm battery could be placed in the satellite phone and I could speak to Sarah wherever she was, usually in the vehicle somewhere. Then I had to tell her our position, the coordinates of which we could read from our GPS; the distance we'd travelled, which our GPS worked out from yesterday's position; our status; our predicted position for tomorrow; and finally anything that needed to be said. Today I told her that we'd done 21 kilometres, Pete was suffering from altitude sickness and please could he speak with one of the doctors. A time was arranged to phone the following morning.

After the scheduled call every day we had a slot to record a 60-second diary message which was put on the race website for the world to hear. This meant that whilst everyone was sitting in a snug warm house eating food of their choice and sleeping in comfortable beds, they could think about how a group of crazed fanatics at the other end of the world were managing to stay alive in tiny vulnerable tents, at high altitude, amid gale force winds in the lowest temperatures on the planet... ostensively just for fun.

My top priority was to get Pete to drink and eat. He wouldn't eat, but did drink a little ginger tea. As I gave him the cup he looked at me with sorrowful eyes. I had seen that look before. Desperate not to let me down, not to let himself down. He curled up and went straight to sleep.

I sat up, wondering. Something was very wrong, but I couldn't quite put my finger on it. Pete had been struggling with exhaustion. He'd been lethargic, irritable and, what worried me more than anything, irrational. Normally he was the most rational person I knew. Maybe he was right and it was the altitude. I'd never thought that we would have problems with it here because of our acclimatisation time, but I knew that sometimes bodies can take five months to adapt properly. Good acclimatisation was one thing sitting still, but quite another continually pushing oneself on the move for long days, pulling a heavy load. He had suffered from altitude sickness before. He knew a lot about it. I remembered when I had suffered severely how confused I'd felt then. It seems to hit people arbitrarily. It reduces the oxygen that is reaching the muscles and the brain, so it's not fun, and his body might be more vulnerable after his recent operations. Was this what our journey was going to be like here?

What could I do about it? I knew that the most important way to help him was with hydration, particularly as we were losing so much water with each breath, here in the dry atmosphere, and with food as basic fuel. But I realised I could also help on a different level. I could give love and, in particular, unconditional love. This felt like the most positive thing to do to give him the most strength. I had to find that place of unconditional love.

Our partnership had always worked with him being the strong one. Suddenly the tables had turned. I had to be the strong one. Tomorrow the tables might turn again. So long as one of us was strong, all would be well.

It had been an intensely frustrating day for us both.

Team Southern Lights had had the worst start imaginable.

Shining Lights

In the morning Pete was worse and in an upset-little-boy space of tears and tantrums. I'd never seen him like this before. He spoke with Doc Ian on the satellite phone, and was advised:

"Try not to be so obsessed with the altitude. Treat it as an energy problem and drink and eat all you can. Relax and enjoy yourself as though you're on holiday."

It seemed to be a prescription for stress-release, but Pete took heed and had a good breakfast and hydrated well. Fingers crossed we would carry on, but gently. We headed out, later than planned, at 10:45am into another beautiful day with the sun shining brightly. It felt just a bit cooler than yesterday.

We decided to adapt the standard routine of stopping every two hours and sitting on the pulk for food and drinks, by interspersing a brief stop every hour for chocolate. We kept bags of small pieces available in our jacket pockets for the purpose. Even so, it was always a struggle to unzip the pocket, open the bag, grip the chocolate with big gloves and work our way through the large tangle of nose and beard icicles to actually find the mouth underneath the face-masks. It always took a while to munch frozen chocolate, so we could only stuff in as much as possible and eat as we continued, but we found that it helped our energy a lot and mentally was something nearer in time to aim for. The main problem was in being able to access my watch through all the different layers to see the time. Sometimes I just guessed, but invariably the time had gone slower than I thought.

We were able to gauge a reasonable sense of time by the sun position, once we'd become accustomed to the sun going around in its southern hemisphere, anti-clockwise way. At least we didn't have to worry about water going down the plughole in the wrong direction. Ah, what I'd give to have water going down a plughole in any direction. The sun moves 15° every hour. So if, for example, my shadow was pointing due south at midday, then by the time my shadow was pointing due east I would know that the sun had moved by 90° and it would be 6pm. Unfortunately, the time of due south shadow changed as we neared the Pole, but we were able to have a pretty good idea. Also it was useful to confirm that we were actually moving in a southerly direction by noting the time. Of course, the sun clock only worked if it was shining.

Today it seemed we had the weather angels on our side. Even so if we had more than 10 minutes sitting on the pulks the slight breeze would get to work and we would become deeply chilled. The options of longer breaks with the wrecked emergency shelter or duvet jackets still seemed such an effort that we stuck with the 10 minute maximum stop. This was not useful at the beginning of the day when one of us was on holiday and sauntering though break times, oblivious to the fact that we could die of cold in the meantime.

After breaks it would take at least 20 minutes to warm up by using the well-choreographed dance routine of windmilling arms, rapid short steps, clawing hands and screwing up face. Then I could relax into my own thoughts.

I started to practise sending unconditional love. I found it similar to sending healing love, which I do every day in my meditation time. I go through a list of family and friends and visualise the energy of blessing and healing as a bubble of white light surrounding them each. It's as though energy comes through me and I just act as a pipe-line, converting high-vibration energy into a state where it can be used if needed. People who aren't used to this process find it strange and of course everyone sees it in their own way. Some find it akin to prayer, but this is the ever-developing method that I have used over many years, and one that suits me.

Unconditional love literally means loving another for who they are regardless of what they do; loving another, but expecting nothing in return. I found it a very heart-based process. Now throughout the day I shot bubbles of unconditional love at Pete every time we set off, I turned around or he said something. It became a fun game.

This began to have an effect on how I felt myself. I would find that if he said something to me that might have previously made me annoyed or frustrated, I didn't react. Now I just laughed to myself, thought unconditional love, and sent a bubble. Then I could deal with whatever it was without the emotion. It was as though I had found a way to raise my vibration or perhaps a way to be in touch with that part of myself that was of a higher vibration.

With this, it also appeared to be a way of being in touch with the shining lights all around – the shining beings of light of Antarctica. The snow was littered with sparkling ice crystals, sometimes catching tiny flashing rainbows, sometimes blazing brilliantly, and the beautiful sastrugi dolphins had clusters of diamond facets in different forms, glinting and gleaming. Even the air was alive with ice crystals, like scintillating star-dust. It was as though the whole landscape was dancing with light from very close up to far out towards the curved horizon, where the clouds seemed to arch and reflect the lustre of the snow. I gasped at what I saw there. High, wispy cloud had formed into the shape of a huge, six-pointed star flowing out as though sending rays of light. The six-pointed figure of balance was like two triangles: one pointing skywards to the heavens, the other pointing straight down to the South Pole. Wow! There was a sign indeed.

The magic was broken as we came upon one of the campsites of the other teams. There was the little ring of snow that had been on the tent valances surrounded by scuffled unnatural lumps and boot tracks, like some long-forgotten burial ground. All of us tried to leave no trace behind, but it was impossible. We would always be careful to squash down the wall built behind the loo pit and cover it up. Human poo waste was the only thing we were allowed to leave behind. It had to be well dug in so that eventually it would be ground by the glacial ice. Along with yellow wee marks in the snow. Sometimes this was almost a friendly thing to come across as signs of other life, but we knew that with the next blizzard these and all evidence of the camp would be wiped off the face of the Antarctic, as though a brief human visit was as ephemeral as the passing clouds.

Mostly, I found I enjoyed the sense of Pete and myself alone in this huge incredible wilderness that holds the end of the world together. It was completely awe-inspiring.

We took it slowly and steadily through the day and thankfully Pete seemed to find more energy and return to his normal self, though he was still becoming short of breath. We had both been shaken by his experience. At the 7:30 sched-call I reported that he was feeling better. I sat on the pulk with my duvet jacket on, but had trouble getting through on the satellite phone. By the time I had finished, my body and particularly my fingers were numb with the cold. It took almost half an hour to do the GPS readings, the sched-call and the diary call. I was strongly of the opinion that it was a good idea to put the tent up at 7:15 every evening so that we could do the sched-call in the shelter of the tent. This meant we had to stay on a 24-hour day. Also, we would have to regulate our skiing-day lengths by rising earlier and earlier in the morning.

I'm not very good in the mornings, even at the best of times. This next one was no exception. Getting up to do a wee was not a problem. Thanks to the Whiz, I was able to operate a pee bottle for the first time in my life. So I could give up wishing I was a man and also, I didn't have to go outside. This, however, wasn't the case in the poo department. The worst moment of the day came early on in the shape of rushing outside, grabbing a shovel and squatting out of the wind behind a snow wall. The fact that there's a nice view all the way to the edge of the Earth didn't really help. Today it was minus 32°C. Colder with wind chill. Colder still exposing a warm bum, but it gets worse. The loo paper is wedges of iced snow (not sure this will ever catch on in British supermarkets). By the time I was back in the tent, the day could only get better.

Our breakfast of oats, powder packs and hot water should have been a happy time. It was important to shove in as much as possible to keep the body going for the day ahead, but we both struggled with it. The trouble was that for some reason I always felt nauseous in the morning (no, not pregnant), and Pete decided after the second day of the acclimatisation trek that knights-in-shining-armour like everything but oats.

Preparing the drinks for the day took time, too. Pete liked a flask of hot chocolate and I liked two small flasks of soup and hot chocolate. Then we had two bottles of Empact water and one of water that we wrapped in duvet jackets to keep from freezing. A pack of day-food each went into the day-packs, along with the rations of cheese and nuts. We were counting out the nuts. Already we would have given everything we had to be able to pop out to the supermarket and buy some more.

Even though we'd woken up at 6:30am, it was 9:00am by the time we were on skis. We would have to get our routine slicker and quicker. We both felt better this morning. Pete had found some energy and I had taped the blisters that had been painful yesterday. There was not a cloud in the sky. After a couple of hours I even took my jacket off. As I was strapping it onto my pulk we spotted something on the horizon. It looked like four red, yellow and black items. All deserts have mirages, of course, so it was obviously a mirage, but after a while this one behaved very oddly and came nearer. It appeared to be a travelling circus. There were four wagon trains with caterpillar-tracked vehicles towing sledged equipment, one of them on a rope 100 metres long. A dozen or so people jumped out and stared at us in amazement. They had thought they had the Antarctic to themselves. They weren't the only ones. The bewilderment was soon broken by warm handshakes.

"How nice to see you. Would you like to come in for a cup of coffee?"

It hadn't said anything in the race rules about not popping in for coffee with circuses should the occasion arise, so how could we refuse? We were led into a large red shed inscribed with "Norwegian-American Antarctic Traverse 2007-2009" where we were entertained with hot drinks and biscuits sitting at a real table, next to a real kitchen. Young scientists in woolly hats and duvet jackets told us what they were up to.

"We're part of a four-year project researching climate change in this part of the Antarctic, to see how it fits into the bigger picture. This is particularly useful for our knowledge about the global relationship between temperature and carbon dioxide, but there's still much that we don't know here."

"What sort of stuff are you doing?"

"The main thing is we're taking ice cores, which are great. They reveal more than 1,000 years of climate history. Our preliminary results suggest that temperatures may actually have been warming here in the past few decades."

"Wow."

"The ice cores are supported by other research including the deep radar which is operated from the isolation hut we're towing behind. This maps the internal layers of the ice-sheet. Beneath us in this area we've found four sub-glacial lakes, liquid because of the heat of the Earth and insulated by two kilometres of ice. We think the lakes are over 100 metres deep. How about that! And here in this flat area the ice-sheet is actually floating on the lakes. It's all really exciting research."

We could have sat there in the shelter all day, not *just* because it was all so interesting, but headed off with a good feeling of nations working together for the betterment of humanity. Also a secure feeling as they had told us that they use a crevasse detector and that our route should be free of crevasses. They'd driven over the ski tracks that we'd been following, but in their place left a nice smooth motorway, so for three kilometres we whizzed along at double the speed. When the tracks diverged we considered following the motorway all the way to the South Pole, but weren't sure how many underground lakes we'd have to visit. Reluctantly we took the rough slow route. Much like driving in Britain, really.

The unscheduled stop had thrown out our routine. We missed a lunchbreak. Fairly soon we were both suffering with low energy. Then the slow pace made me feel deeply cold, my shoulders aching and sore. I didn't feel like eating and couldn't seem to get warm. The body machine was so low on food and water I was virtually running on empty. I was doing all the things that I'd told Pete not to do. Part of the problem was that neither of us particularly wanted to eat our day-food. We craved savoury foods and the nuts and cheese went too quickly. So we stuffed in chocolate and liquid, recognising with surprise and concern how "on the edge" we seemed to be. As long as one of us had that awareness, then we'd be okay. If that awareness went, then we could be in trouble; confusion and hypothermia can set in quickly. Hopefully we would manage things better as time went on. At least we knew how important it was to watch out for the other one.

"Why don't you listen to your MP3 player?" Pete suggested, "It'll stir you up."

"Okay, thanks. I'll try," I replied shooting him a bubble of unconditional love. He was right. Within a few minutes I went from feeling lousy to feeling great. What a difference. Due to my technical incompetence my little machine plays what comes rather than what I chose. Generally it's a system that works very well. I let the universe decide what I need. Today it went for the selection of positive songs that my son Paul had put on for me. Perfect. Very soon I was striding along in time to the music in a new world, feeling positive, and then, like plugging into a power socket, I suddenly felt in touch again with the shining lights that were all around, in the snow, in the air, in the sastrugi formations, but this time I was an integral part of them, almost as though I was them. It led me to understand that Antarctica with all its purity is a huge reservoir of light for the Earth; I could see a picture of the planet being held from its base as if by a hand of light.

With this revelation I became aware that I was observing the whole of the Earth as I looked around into the vast expanse of white through the forms in the snow. Not only were there dolphins and whales, jumping and smiling in the surf, but forests in the striated bark of the trees, deserts in the sand-dunes with sidewinder snakes leaving their trails, the open cells of a luscious grass stem, the wrinkled face of an old man, the soft folds of a new-born baby, and animals of the Earth, from slugs to hippos, lion-cubs to swans, beetles to crocodiles. Even those from eons long gone, of volcanic lava sweeping through mudflats stalked by plodding dinosaurs with pterodactyls flying. They were all represented in the shining oneness of the snow all around, the oneness of life itself. I beheld it all, privileged to be part of it and felt like I was shining, too.

Unfortunately, however good a time my mind was having, I couldn't get away from the fact that my body was wandering across the coldest place on Earth.

Cracking of the Shell

It was the practicalities of putting the tent up that brought me back to the reality of our physical situation. By then I was aware that Pete was struggling inwardly. He was out of character again, being exceptionally bossy.

My problems continued through the night. I couldn't sleep. Pete had rolled right over to my side of the tent, snoring. I wondered how the teams with three guys were coping, and when the sun was shining it was still *hot* in the sleeping bags. Crazy! When the alarm went off I tried hard but couldn't find a good enough reason to get out of my bag. I felt like a hopeless wreck with no energy. Every bit of my body ached. I refused to move. Pete patiently prepared all the water bottles and then patched his leather gloves. What had happened to my go-go, get-out-in-record-time man? It appeared he was still on holiday. I was helped by a thought that eventually drifted into my awareness — the crystals and the Peace Messages. Ah. For them I would attempt to wake up and start the day, though not before stupidly spilling a cup of precious hot water. Pete put his boots on the wrong feet. Was this the dynamic couple that thought they could do anything?

I caught the edge of a feeling that my mind couldn't quite grasp. That we were both being stripped down of the shell that normally held our individual selves together. Of the way that we usually coped with life. We were fighting to hold onto it, but it was going to be stripped down whether we liked it or not.

Cold Hands, Warm Heart

We were blessed with sun again, but each day the temperature was dropping and there always seemed to be something that we were coming up against. Today for a few hours we battled over heavy fields of sastrugi. Pete was fighting exhaustion and the slow times left us deeply cold. The sitting lunchbreaks every two hours couldn't come quickly enough, but the whole process was such an effort with an achy, seized-up body and big gloves. First unclip harness and fiddle with zips to be able to wee (as quickly as possible!). Then align the skis and sit, or rather collapse, onto my pulk. I now carried both of our day-food packs and drinks, so it was a matter of unstrapping the cover and finding them. Each thing was so hard to do that I found I had to really push myself to be bothered with any of it. Like getting into the drinks. Invariably the lids on my little flasks and the bottle tops would be stuck and it would be knight-in-shining-armour to the rescue, but I didn't like to ask him. He was slowly fighting every step, too. It was good to sit close and feel him next to me for a few moments, both with our backs to the wind. It was hard to find the energy to turn and look into his face, but I knew what I'd see there anyway. Underneath the pushed-up goggles and mask, amongst the enveloping growth of ice, would be a drawn expression devoid of vitality. Today he just quietly said:

"This is definitely the toughest thing I've ever done."

It only needed one brush of a gloved hand to communicate that we were there for each other. By the time we had packed everything away, strapped up the pulk and reclipped the harness it was a relief to start moving the skis. I wrinkled my nose and screwed-up my face to bring the blood-flow in and rid it of that feeling of ice pins and needles. I knew that it would take the next half an hour to warm up the body and be able to feel the hands again. Sometimes I almost dreaded stopping.

Once after a lunchbreak there was a rare couple of minutes skiing alongside and energy to squander on silliness.

"D'you remember that time when we first met and I promised I'd follow you to the ends of the Earth?"

"Yeah."

"Well, I've changed my mind."

"Shut up!"

As always, we then fell back one behind the other.

I couldn't wait to return to my own mind games, practising shooting unconditional love and the beautiful thoughts that continued to sustain me whilst the body plodded, one ski in front of the other, forever onwards.

The next day my meditation kept me going for hours with a colour-cleanse. I went through red, orange, yellow, green, blue, indigo and violet, spending a long happy time picturing everything lovely that I could think of in each colour. I imagined myself full of the colour and then letting it go, knowing that the process was cleansing and balancing each of the energy centres in my body. Afterwards I wound up all the colours and spun them around until they became white, as white as the white world around me, and filled myself with white light. Now I could enjoy the thought that my Antarctica was made up of a plethora of glorious colours.

Then I fell into thinking about my sons Paul, Scottie and Marco and picturing the times we would have on my return. It made me emotional and tears slipped out and became droplets of ice on my cheeks, freezing so fast that they didn't even mist up the goggles. I felt defenceless. I wondered if this, like the fear, was part of the cracking and breaking of the shell of self that would allow a state of vulnerability, so as to be in the right energy for the peace ceremony job.

For the next three hours of the day I switched on my MP3 player by pressing through into an inner pocket. I had put the earphones on in the tent ready for use. It would have been far too fiddly to do outside. Today the universe decided that I would listen to the Dalai Lama. His words of compassion, inner disarmament and gentleness were especially profound in this awesome landscape. They carried me along until sched-call time. I was learning that to concentrate on my mind rather than my body was a considerable help.

I had no idea how Pete was managing to struggle through the mire of exhaustion in his own private hell. It wouldn't go away. I couldn't think of anyone else I knew that wouldn't have given up, but we were pleased that at last we were slowly building up our hours and distance. Today we had covered 31 kilometres.

In the morning I woke up with a sense of excitement, feeling that I was now ready for some sort of insight guidance to begin in my meditation times. I prepared for the day as quickly as possible, keen to get going early, but Pete seemed to have reverted into another space with irrational outbursts that made no sense at all and was determined not to be hurried. What a strange role reversal, I thought, thinking of all the months of his attempts to speed me up.

"Love you. All is well," I encouraged.

"Shut up," he growled. A call for a shot of unconditional love.

Packing up, loading the pulks, striking the tent and preparing for the off was now something that we were quite used to, but even so it always took a lot of energy, helped by having chocolate pieces ready as we started skiing. Then there was the mental preparation for being with the cold. Often it took half an hour or so to settle down into the skiing rhythm. Today Pete never reached that place. It wasn't long before I heard a shout of, "Stop!"

He came up alongside and collapsed full length on to my pulk. I unclipped my harness and quickly, though awkwardly on skis, walked round to him. He was lying motionless. I couldn't see his face. Placing my hand on his shoulder, I called softly

"Pete!"

There was no reaction. I called again. Still no reaction. What was I meant to do now?

"C'mon, Baby, we've got to keep going. You'll get hypothermia if you don't move." Baby was a name I saved for dire circumstances. This was a dire circumstance. The seconds turned into interminable minutes. I lost sense of time, but no reaction. I didn't know how long he'd been lying there but I did know that I had to do something urgently to get him to move. His core temperature would be plummeting. It was only a matter of minutes before we could be in serious trouble. Even though the sun was shining and the wind light, the temperature must be around minus 35°C. Somehow I had to get through to him.

"Pete!" I shouted. "Listen to me. I'm going to put the tent up, and I'm going to phone and get them to come and pick us up and take us home. Is that what you want?" I knew that was the last thing in the world he wanted. If anything was going to get through to him it would be that. I continued, "Either you keep going or we get picked up."

He sat up, "I don't think I can give any more," he said, shaking his head despairingly "I'm never *ever* doing anything like this again."

Relieved, I handed him some chocolate and dug into the pulk for a drink bottle for him. Thank goodness my reasoning had finally stirred him. But then he said, "I've paid 42 grand for this and I'm jolly well not going to waste it." So that's what it had been. Ah, the power of money.

We continued slowly. By the time we'd had our 2:30 break he seemed to have stashed his demons and was into go-mode.

My energy had been all over the place and I felt that my vibration would be too low for any insight guidance today, but I settled down into my meditation routine. When I came to the affirmations, I changed it. Usually I go through a whole list of useful attributes such as strength, fitness, health, positivity, lovingness and repeat each one many times like, "I am strong in body, I am strong in mind, I am strong in spirit, I am strong," and I try and hold that sense. Today, believing it would help Pete too, I converted it to,"*We* are strong in body, *we* are strong in mind, *we* are strong in spirit."

It seemed to be this that enabled an insight to be apparent: *"Be open to the path ahead."*

Well that sounded simple enough. Before me stretched the clear marks of the little ski-trail that we were following south. It would remain until the wind returned and ate it away. The lovely thing was that because it stretched out across the vast sparkling land to the distant horizon, it always touched the sky. I turned to look at my pulk, Khandro the Tibetan sky dancer. Yes, I was open to the path ahead. In true Tibetan spirit, in which all experience becomes the path, we were taking the trail that leads to the sky.

At sched-call time we were pleased to report good mileage again. We were making steady progress. Given time, nothing, however hard we were struggling, would stop us following the path.

But Sarah dropped a bombshell.

"Tony's passing you two in the middle of the night with the vehicles. He's going to pick you up. Then you'll be whizzed up to the checkpoint and we want you to set off and break trail in front of the race."

So much for the path ahead.

Egbert the Ego

My ego is called Egbert. There's been trouble with him before. He's the one who thinks he's the best and knows all the answers. He's also the one who causes all the pain. Like in the Arctic. When we had been stopped from doing that race it had been Egbert who had jumped up and down, furious and disappointed. It had taken a long time for him to quieten down. When he did it was possible to see that spending a couple of weeks with the Inuit people and then flying up to the magnetic North Pole to conduct our peace ceremony had in fact been a much better outcome than being on the race itself.

Now here he was again. He was most indignant. "I don't wanna be picked up," he yelled. "I want to complete the South Pole Race under my own steam. That's why I entered and trained so hard. I've given everything I've got to do this. It's really important. What about my self esteem? And what will people think? How can I go home not having done the thing, after all this. For the second time, too. It's just like in the Arctic."

Shut up, Egbert.

"It's not fair. Just because the time for the race has had to be cut short. And because they happen to be going past. It's too early to be picked up. I know we can do it. We're just working through our difficulties and getting into a good routine. The weather's great. We just need a little more time. We're already doing more distance per day than most expeditions for goodness sake, even than Amundsen did with his dogs..."

Egbert, SHUT UP!

There was nothing we could do about it. We were falling behind the race safety net, where-in rescue was possible if necessary. There was nothing else the organisers could do. They had to put our safety paramount and they couldn't manage the logistics if a team was too far behind. I had asked Sarah if we could treat it as a senior handicap. "Absolutely," she said. That made me feel a little better. Not a lot, but a little. "You're still in the race," she'd said. "It's just that you can't win."

It was not easy facing the disappointment. Though we had known it possible, we had tried to ignore it, so were in a bit of a state of shock. We prepared the gear and wriggled into our sleeping bags, but I couldn't sleep. One ear was listening out for the sound of a vehicle, which we didn't want to hear and didn't fit in with this beautiful wilderness. The other was trying to work it all out. We had been battling, sure, but this place was still awe-inspiringly magnificent and part of me didn't want to be taken away from that by being involved with people and human machines. However, it did help that we had been through the disappointment before and this time we would get to continue the race. Egbert didn't have a leg to stand on.

Right. I would try and be accepting and open to the path ahead. No doubt somehow this was all evolving as it should. It was just that I couldn't see it at the moment. Then something else came to mind. It seemed so long ago now, but it must have been just before leaving England. Dorje, the monk who works with the Gesar Foundation had said, "To allow the universal energy to work through you, it is necessary to surrender... to put yourself aside."

"Good night, Egbert."

There was no reply.

He was probably out with Pete's ego, drowning his sorrows.

Senior Handicap

It was the vibration I felt first. Then heard the sound of engines. Rushing out of the tent I saw the dark outlines of two of the Arctic trucks with trailers, roof-racks and pick-up space all piled high with equipment, though with room for pulks to be strapped on top. One of them roared towards us and sputtered to a halt. There was a whiff of petrol and motor oil. Tony and Doc Deirdre jumped out. The cavalry had arrived.

They'd had a long, slow and extremely tiring journey from the end of the acclimatisation trek, with lots of vehicle problems, and trouble with crevasses. They had resolved this by putting Doc Deirdre out in front on the end of a rope as crevasse detector. When she disappeared they knew there was a crevasse. No doubt it would be written up in medical journals as a breakthrough diagnostic technique furthering the cause of scientific research.

We were about to have a taste of support-team living. Travelling in the vehicles was surprisingly slow and frustrating. The air was kept low in the tyres to spread the load and give traction, but it made for a very bumpy ride. There was almost no leg-room in the back, causing my knees to seize up, and I immediately felt car-sick. These weren't the sort of Antarctic problems that I had anticipated. I wished I were still on skis. I told myself not to be silly. We were warm and that was more important than anything.

After a three-hour drive we were reunited with the other half of the support crew and their two trucks. The one known as Bruce was jacked up with a wheel-axle problem. It was great to see everybody and chat. The camera crews were frustrated that because of the vehicle problems they hadn't been able to film the teams, but we gleaned that at the non-senior end of the race there was an exciting tussle going on. Missing Link and QinetiQ were battling it out neck and neck for first place. They, like all the other teams, were covering huge distances and skiing for long hours. It was anybody's guess who would be first into the checkpoint. We weren't meant to hear these things, being racers, but at least we learnt that they were all okay.

We put our tent up for a while and Doc Deirdre came to check Pete's body. She used a pulse oximeter to determine the oxygen saturation of his blood. Fixing a little clip onto one of his fingers the percentage then came up on a monitor. Figures of 95-100 percent are accepted as fine, though oxygen levels are expected to be a bit lower at high altitude. Below 90 percent indicates a state of hypoxia, where the body is deprived of adequate oxygen supply and cannot function normally. Both extreme cold and physical activity exacerbate this as they increase the body's demand for oxygen. This can manifest in many ways, but one of the obvious symptoms is extreme fatigue. Pete's reading showed up as 87 percent.

"Each of us reacts differently to altitude," she said. "You may not have adapted in the expected way. Your lungs are having to work overtime which explains your shortness of breath, and the cold, dry air makes it harder for your respiratory system to utilise the oxygen. My advice, of course, is to rest, which is not what you want to hear, but what you can do is make sure you always eat and drink for the hour ahead, so your body is not so depleted."

I offered a finger. My reading was okay at 98 percent, but I tried to take note of Deirdre's comments. We needed to find how to give our bodies their requirements without teetering "on the edge" so much. It appeared that, for whatever reason, we were stuck with having Pete's body working at a low oxygen level. A five percent lowering of oxygen saturation is meant to be the equivalent of being at an additional 1,000 metres of altitude. This showed that Pete's body was operating at the equivalent of 2,000 metres higher than mine. We were now at an altitude of 2,700 metres, which was 3,600 metres with the lower pressure. So he was in his own space pushing himself to the limit every day at 5,600 metres. Not only his lungs but his muscles, brain and everything were oxygen depleted. My goodness! How was he managing to keep going at all?

Chocolate was an answer. It was the food that helped us more than any other. We devoured vast quantities of the nutty variety. Not only does it give a boost of caffeine, fat and sugar, resulting in wakefulness, heat and energy, but it stimulates the production of serotonin and endorphins, creating the "feel-good" magic. We had a problem with our chocolate, however. It came in large cannon-ball like lumps thanks to the South African heat. So now, with a little time to pass, we set-to with multi-tools to have a cannon-ball breakdown session.

The vehicle breakdown session ended around midnight, so we packed up and strapped our pulks on top of the oil drums on one of the trailers and set off for a 14-hour, bone-rattling, knee-hugging car-sick journey. I was sitting with Kenny, Sarah and Alexis which was special, particularly as we could have nice conversations, but it was mostly about food. I was coming to realise that conversation in the Antarctic is nearly always about food. Why couldn't people talk about something else? It wasn't very positive for my car-sick stomach.

Then I was surprised. Sarah asked me if I would like some noodles. I thought I'd better force something down so accepted. Wow. Yum. It was just what I needed. My body decided that it would do anything I asked of it so long as it was fed noodles. I thought of the hundreds of miles that we had to ski on day-food and yearned for the large pile of noodles that we had spurned in Cape Town. Crazy. Normally I don't even like noodles, but then I understood why conversation is always about food in the Antarctic, and realised that sometimes you have to feel things through the deep core of your being to understand them. It's amazing what you can learn from noodles.

At last we drew up at a piece of snow that looked more or less like every other piece of snow, except that it was at 86° south, 21° east. This was the checkpoint. I was in a lack-of-sleep daze. The vast white desert that sometimes feels so full was now empty, bleak and desolate, but it was soon transformed by our little camp with its green bell-shaped communications tent and handful of smaller red ones, and there was the noise of voices and the banging of gear being moved around. Humans clinging to life against all the odds. Once we'd dragged our pulks to a spot and erected the tent we hurriedly sorted food from our resupply bag and filled fuel bottles ready to ski off in the morning. The good weather seemed to have broken. It was colder than we had yet experienced, a keen wind was blowing and low cloud was gathering from the east.

We slept for 12 hours and felt like we could do the same again, but there was some shouting going on. Exciting news. The lead team was coming in. We looked to the north and there they were. It was a team of two, it must be Missing Link. The Norwegians had beaten the British to the halfway point. They walked in between the heavily flapping sponsor flags that had been put out to welcome them, holding their hands up together in triumph. They had skied almost continuously for two days with no sleep and only one quick tent stop to melt snow for water. They had managed to sneak past QinetiQ, when they were having a brief tent stop. What an achievement. Rune had really bad blisters and both of them were shattered, but elated. At least now there was the compulsory 24-hour stop to recuperate. They came by our tent:

"We think you're amazing," Stian said. "I can't see my parents doing what you have. If I'm half as active as you are at your age I shall be delighted."

"Hey hang on, we're meant to be congratulating you," I said, hugging him. How sweet he was to be thinking of us when they were the ones that had done so well. As they headed off no doubt to sleep for 20 hours, I called after them, "You're an inspiration to the youth of the world." So far they were impressively upholding Amundsen's status.

Team QinetiQ were only four hours behind them, though, and the other teams would all be in the checkpoint within the next two days. It was still anybody's race to win.

But we had to leave, though not before Sarah let us see another batch of encouraging emails so we could head out with the knowledge that so many were enjoying the diary transmissions and thinking of us. Pete was particularly pleased to hear from his children, Claire, Graeme, Caroline and Anna. My brother Graham wrote, "Mum's well and now accepts that it's quite a normal thing to be walking to the South Pole in January. And isn't it amazing what the 60s bus pass now includes...". I stored the emails in my mind to enjoy later as I was keen to get moving. I felt really cold. My toes had gone numb and my fingers weren't far behind. It was minus 33°C and hanging around wasn't good. We left rubbish and resupply bag, pulled down the tent, packed the pulks and clipped into our skis.

Deirdre came to give us a big hug and took a picture of us. As she did so, I managed to somehow slip and fall down heavily on my back. She and Kenny rushed to pick me up. How kind they were. I felt bathed in warmth from them both and it helped lift and calm my energy which was cold and stressed. It seemed to be a reminder that breaking the shell of dignity and becoming vulnerable allows something beautiful to come through.

"Make sure you *enjoy* the race" Kenny advised. "We will find you in 10 days' time to give you your resupply for the last six days." He was giving us special treatment. He was looking after "the olds" as he called us. We appreciated not having to pull 16 full days of food and fuel.

Tony was waiting at the sponsor flag markers. "You can do it," he said, putting his arms around us both. "You've got 375 kilometres to go in 16 days. That's 24 kilometres a day. See you at the South Pole by midday on the 28th. I don't want to have to pick you up again."

"Yes, we'll be there. To the South Pole and beyond!" I proclaimed, punching the air.

And we were off... heading south.

Of course we would be there. What could possibly stop us?

Cold Hands

In spite of our words to Tony I couldn't seem to motivate myself. We had only lost two days of skiing, but, as Egbert insisted on pointing out, it was two years of dreams. We were still on the race, but it was different. There was something vital that circumstances had taken out of our hands, leaving a dull, cold emptiness. The South Pole still seemed as far away as ever; I couldn't touch it with my mind. It just floated illusively like something that would always be in the future.

It did feel good to be back on skis, though, just the two of us, in control of our own destiny. We looked forward to seeing the other teams as they overtook us, but now we were in the lead, for however brief a time. This meant, of course, that there were no tracks to follow. It was a whole different ballgame. We couldn't even use shadow directions; the sun was intermittent and the contrast had dropped, but navigation was one of Pete's specialities, so he was happy. The checkpoint sleep and lots of food had done him good and he was quite his old self. He quickly went out in front wearing the compass rig, adjusted by the deviation of 46°W from magnetic south. This figure, which we read from the GPS, was to decrease as we came nearer and nearer to the geographic Pole. After a while he worried that the compass wasn't working correctly as the wind was in the wrong place and we veered over to the east. Then checking with the GPS, he had to accept that the wind is not always constant in spite of what we had been told. He went back to trusting the compass and following its little arrow south, sorry that we had made a bit of a wiggly trail for the others.

I was happy to leave the navigation to him. Feeling tired even before we left, I was finding the reloaded pulk very heavy. It kept jarring and pulling me back as we crossed rough sastrugi. I hadn't laced my boots tight enough and my right ankle kept going over. Tying laces was not something that I felt I was brave enough to do during a break because of cold hands, so I made a mental note to get it right tomorrow, and I might swap the skis around. They were meant to be one for right and one for left, but I found that the "Harmony" ski was more stable than the "Peace on Earth" ski, whichever foot it was on. I made a note to sort out "Peace on Earth," too.

After a while, the circulation returned to my numb toes. I was used to that with the hands. I had put on an extra layer of contact gloves today, underneath my double layer Norwegian mitts. I liked to fix my gloves on well in the tent and then not take them off for the day. That worked as long as I had the wrist toggle closed so there was air space around the fingers that could warm up. Pete worked on a system of using thick leather gloves and having over-gloves that he pulled on and off when doing different things.

Whatever the glove system, after a 10 minute break the hands were always numb. This was something I found scary, but I knew somewhere around half an hour after we were moving again, with lots of shaking and clawing of hands, that the circulation would return. Frostbite was an ever present threat though, should we let our guard down and allow the fingers to reach a white state that wouldn't go away.

The body has its own survival mechanism. When struck by extreme cold, it withdraws all the heat from the extremities to protect the core organs such as the heart. This is particularly so after eating, as the digestive system demands heat. The hands give their life blood. There is a critical point beyond which it will not return. There is a race to generate further heat by the movement of the body, so warmth can return to the hands, but by all systems of the body working together there is survival.

Whilst struggling with cold hands after our second lunchbreak and somewhat despondent, I went into an empty sort of a space in my mind. An insight came through:

"By working together there will be survival."

That's so simple, so basic, I thought. Of course I know that. Pete and I were out here in the middle of nowhere totally dependent on each other. Then I saw; it wasn't just about our tiny team, it was about the Earth. Just like the body, the Earth has its own survival mechanism. Only by all systems of the Earth working together will there be survival, and humanity is an integral part of the Earth's systems. We cannot be separated. We have to work in harmony with the Earth, not against it.

At the moment we are out of balance. Humanity needs an extra third of a planet to sustain the resources that it is using. If everyone consumed at the current level of some of the western world that would be *three* extra planets needed. Things are urgent. We are borrowing from our children. The race for the peace and harmony of the Earth is the important race.

Trudging on across the snow, I now felt much more motivated. Carrying our Peace Messages was a little part of something huge, making a difference to the future of our Earth.

I knew how important it was to find positive thoughts. It made such a difference to the whole process of staying strong inwardly, feeling able to cope and not buckling. In some ways it was the best protection against the savage, relentless cold. It was just hard to hold on to. I kept drifting off track. I remembered in a corner of my mind what Beverley had said. He's an angelic kind of friend who appears when there's a problem, offers wonderful advice and then disappears, leaving the impression that there is always help there, that we only have to ask and be open to the answers. "Get your thoughts right," he had said, "and the physical *must* follow. It's just like pulling a pulk." Yes, energy follows thought. Do not forget, I told myself.

Cold Hands, Warm Heart

There is little more mind-changing in an Antarctic day than the moment of warmth. This tends to come after the tent is up, gear sorted, stoves lit, snow melted, food prepared and with the stove in the inner section. It's wonderful. Suddenly all things seem possible again. I tried to linger over the evening meal, but knew that I would feel better if I could fit in a quick wash. Plus, there was always mending to be done. I was so grateful that I didn't have to worry about contact lenses. My eyes worked brilliantly. Pete had to operate much of the time without his glasses because of misting and icing up, but he could see sufficiently (not quite sure why he kept calling me Liz).

All too soon it was time to turn off the little valve that let the petrol from the fuel bottle through to the stove. When there was no sun like today the temperature immediately plummeted. I put on my hat with "resolute" written on it. Not only did I hope that some of that characteristic might permeate through to my brain, but I liked the pink and purple colouring and it had a good flap to pull down over my eyes to sleep in. We put our full water bottles, still hot, into the sleeping bags. This was so we would have body temperature water to drink through the night and on waking, but even more precious was the fact that it took the iciness away from the sleeping bag. Also we chucked in various items of clothing that we weren't wearing, such as socks, boot inners and gloves. After a lightning goodnight hug, Pete pulled his hat low over his face, said as always, "Don't stay up too late writing," and was fast asleep before I had written the first two words in my diary.

The next day, the wind chill temperature was close to minus 40°C again. I made my way out of the tent and winced as the wind hit my face, prompting me to pull down my goggles and face mask. There was a half-hearted sun and one fluffy cloud. It wasn't long before heavy cloud came, making it fractionally less cold, but then we could barely tell snow from sky.

It was my turn to have the compass rig and be in front. I quite liked the idea of the focus of the arrow heading

south, though it seemed to jump all over the place with
my movement and I found it really hard to watch it as well
as the way ahead. It was wonderful that we had the wind
behind us today. What a difference that made to the face,
though more often than not I still had to keep my hood up.
In spite of all the layers underneath, there always seemed
to be a gap on my neck where the icy wind could penetrate.
I knew that I had to concentrate on the navigation which
left little opportunity for the escape of mind time, but I very
quickly zoomed through my meditation routine. At the point
of dedicating the day to the healing of the Earth an insight
snuck in:

"As effort creates heat, so effort in the name of love creates light."

There was no time then to process the thought. I had to
focus on the arrow, though I kept having a feeling that I
wanted to go further over to the west, as though I was being
drawn there. "Be rational girl," I told myself, "you're the
navigator today." I should have been more rational still. It
wasn't until a 3pm lunchbreak that I checked our position
against the GPS. Oh bother, we were way off our longitude
coordinate of 21° east. I was cross with myself. It was a
harsh lesson in always checking our position against the
GPS. Now it meant a nightmare journey at a more easterly
direction traversing the line of sastrugi that appeared to have
grown into never-ending fields of bomb-blasted volcanic
eruptions. Finding a very wiggly way through haphazard
ditches and hillocks here, there and everywhere, hauling
what now seemed like an even heavier pulk behind. The
only good thing about it was that all the extra effort made us
really warm. Though this also meant that the wind now hit
us on the left of our faces, which made things much harder.
I should have recognised the wind direction earlier. In this
area the wind generally did come from the east as the ground
was slightly higher and the katabatic effect meant that it
roared from the highest ground wildly down to the coast,
uninterrupted across hundreds of miles.

After a tough 10 hour struggle we were pretty much back
onto our correct longitude, having covered the planned 24

kilometres and made camp. Yes, whatever the problems we would do our 24. What a relief it was to read out the details on the sched-call, but the satisfaction it gave was so short-lived that we could barely catch it as it roared like the wind on its way though.

Sarah had another bomb-shell for us.

"You can't go straight to the Pole. The U.S. exclusion zone means that you'll have to go on a bearing towards 88° south, 20° west. Only then can you go due south into the Pole."

What! To say that we weren't happy was an understatement. It meant that we had to go west by nearly 40°. Pete worked out that it would add 60 kilometres to our total distance. This meant doing five kilometres extra every day to be able to reach the Pole in the required time. Five kilometres might not sound much on paper, but we knew that at the end of a strenuous day in these conditions it was like adding a marathon. We would in all likelihood miss seeing any of the others who we presumed would mostly be able to follow the same line from the checkpoint. We felt totally out on a limb and like we'd just wasted two days of effort in the wrong direction.

We had known that there was a clean-air exclusion sector near the Pole. Fair enough. It was important for scientific enquiry, but we had been told that we could ski through it although the vehicles could not except in the case of an emergency. Why hit us with this now? Something was going on. It was acutely frustrating not knowing what. The fact that I had wanted to go further west all day didn't help at all. So much for being in control of our own destiny.

We both felt stressed, but there was nothing for it but to regroup our focus and head out the next day in a new direction. We decided to take a trajectory a little more west than the direct line, hoping to pick up the trail of the others at some point and reach the new longitude as soon as possible.

It was colder today. The brutal wind brought the wind chill temperature down to minus 42°C and had been busy in the night burying our pulks with spindrift. After a bright start the visibility went leaving little definition, just a heavy greyness of ice and sky, sky and ice enveloping us. It reflected how we felt. Pete had the compass rig and led. He was suffering from a painful back and ankle, and felt overcome by exhaustion from the start, so was slow. This contributed to our coldness. Even though I wore my thick thermals I still had to work hard all day jiggling my hands and holding them low on the sticks so that the blood could flow downwards and keep the numbness at bay. However, I enjoyed the fact that I could follow and not have to navigate. Also I could spend time in my meditation. It was whilst I was going through affirmations that an insight flowed in:

"Repeat 108 times – I am a shining being of light and all things are possible."

I wondered why I should do that. I looked around, but there was no clue from the frozen grey scene. I worked through it, then just for good measure, I did it again. It gave a wonderfully uplifting sense of positivity. I wanted to hold onto it but it was like a beautiful floating bubble just passing by. Searching my memory I found something that helped to explain it, something that Beverley had said. "Everyone is always accompanied by shining beings of light, including their own."

It would have been nice to have shared the experience with Pete at a chocolate break, but it was not easy to convey even down-to-earth words like, "Here, take this," in our low-energy state. Anyway, I might have received back something like, "You've gone bananas." He was fighting his own exhaustion battle. In spite of this he had done a brilliant job, following our new diagonal line, keeping the sastrugi angle consistent. At last we were rewarded by some flatter ice to weave through, but we couldn't help feeling dejected at the thought of being away on a different path from everyone else.

Even Gaius was looking tired. Gradually over the days he had fallen further and further forward, so that his beak was dangerously near the ice. Often he head-butted the sastrugi. Now his toes were actually scratching along it as we went. I would have to do something about this. When the tent was up I went to redo his harness. This was not possible with my mitts on. I took them off and in my contact gloves tried to undo the string. Ice daggers struck my hands like lightening, followed immediately by numbness. I managed, in what can have only been for a moment, to untie it with leaden fingers and then rush into the tent. I couldn't work on the jobs of laying out the mats and kit and preparing the meal. Nor could I sort out all the ice that was all over my duvet jacket and day-sack due to a leaked Empact bottle. I held my hands in my armpits and then shook them for quite a while until, painfully, the circulation returned. I berated myself for being so stupid. I wouldn't have taken my outer gloves off if the tent hadn't been so close, but it was a sharp reminder that this is not a natural human environment.

We were being allowed to tiptoe across this harsh land. It was indeed a privilege to be experiencing this kingdom of the wind, this raw unfettered wilderness, but skis and sticks, pulks and tents, stoves, sleeping bags and windproof clothing were enabling us to live here "on the edge" before we had to fall back into civilisation. Then, maybe then, I would be able to speak warmly of how utterly awesome our dear Earth's freezer is. Right now all I could think was cold... cold... everything is so, so cold.

But cold combined with dryness makes things brittle. That's when they can snap.

The Struggle Holds the Pearl

I don't like the cold, I thought, as we skied the next day. The wind had dropped a bit, but it was little compensation. It felt like it was even colder than yesterday. There was heavy low cloud. Sometimes we could only see a few metres in front. Sometimes it was to as far as where the horizon should be, but sky and snow all merged together. We were entombed in a frigid grey world that sat oppressively over us. It seemed to penetrate right through all the clothes, bringing a heavy chill to my bones.

I was wearing two thermal tops, a fleece layer and a sleeveless fleece underneath my windproof jacket. I soon became hot which meant an energy drop, and we stopped to undo each other's under-arm zips. It was so hard to get it right. At a lower altitude we had stayed warm all day. Now too much warmth only seemed to last for half an hour, then it was gone, eaten by the cold monster. There was a critical skiing speed below which we became really cold. In these very heavy sastrugi conditions and low visibility this was hard to maintain. Our bodies had deteriorated. We were living closer to "the edge". I could see it in the drawn expression of Pete's eyes and in the way his exhaustion came on. Our energy was directed by the sleep, food and drink we had recently had. Being "on the edge" was like balancing scales. We had to keep the input on the "plus" side. Mostly we were treading the line at the tipping point. I knew we hadn't eaten enough breakfast. It was so hard to force it down through the nausea. Then I had dragged my feet about going out, part of me hoping that a delay might make it all go away. Even so, we had set off early, determined to do our distance for the day.

It was my turn for the compass rig. I didn't like wearing it, as it was just one more piece of kit to cope with around the body. Thank goodness we hadn't had to wear the climbing harness and crevasse rescue gear. I didn't know how I'd cope with that. It'd be hard enough to put on out here let alone operate. I was struggling with the navigation and trying to take a straight line. Today it was impossible to tell what was ahead – because of the flat light there was no definition of form. Whether it was a knee-high sastrugi stretching out or a dip to crash into, whether we were going uphill or downhill, it was all the same. Just wait and see and try and react to what arrived underneath the skis, then yank the pulk to follow, tossing and twisting as though on a stormy sea.

Every time my mind wandered, I found I'd gone considerably off to the right, too far west of our bearing. I seemed to have a natural-right tendency. Maybe it's because I'm too right-brained. Pete coming behind was backing me up with the hand compass. Every few minutes he had to shout "Left!" This was supposed to be his day to have a break from concentrating on the navigation, but I was so hopeless it wasn't happening. I was putting more pressure on him. It was intensely frustrating, and I was making such slow progress. I felt as though I was going round in circles.

This was compounded by irrational thoughts that were going round and round in my head. I knew that everyone else must be following a nice track like we'd had in the early part of the race, and here we were, out on a limb and separate. This idea became stuck in my mind and couldn't get out, until it headed into a negative downwards spiral.

It was snowing now. Lightly, but enough to make visibility worse, like the blurring edge of a cloud, allowing my mind to drift further... I don't like the cold. So what am I doing here? I don't like the cold. My body seizes up. My knees ache and act like they're stuck in a freezer. My hands, well there's a thing: they lose their bendability and forget they're attached to my brain, and anyway my left hand only has two fingers that work sensibly. Even at the equator, the others won't bend. They've been like that for 20 years now, ever since I discovered that it's exciting to hang on a rock face just by the fingertips and feel the adrenalin, looking down to a long fall... come on fingers, you can do it... hold my body weight, get those feet helping quick, they're the ones that should be taking the weight... ah, the joy of the flow of the movement upwards, the dance of body and rock to the music of get-it-right-or-die. Was it just the focus I loved? Being forced to live in the moment, or the fear beforehand and the release afterwards? Was it the togetherness, the coordination, the communication with the warm rock... ah, that word again... warm.

I don't like the cold. So what am I doing here in the middle of the Antarctic at minus who-knows-what and on a race, for goodness sake. I never wanted to race, what am I doing on a race to the South Pole? We'll never make it. We're much too slow. I just want to disappear into a black hole in the middle of this white land and be engulfed by it all.

Let go, it seemed to echo... let go... let go. You've been wound up, holding the whole thing so tightly for so many months, battling all the odds, forcing it to happen. You've held it so tight, day after day, being so strong and positive and enthusiastic, through thick and thin, through blizzard and extreme cold, keeping ahead of the fear. You don't have to cling to it. You can let go.

I turned to look for Pete who was waiting for me to read the compass, to get the direction right, so he didn't have to shout at me. Why was I going round in circles? Of course it's the whiteout... or is it grey? More like a murky leaden white, not the shining white that I love when the sun's out, the precious sun that brings up the rainbows and sparkles of magic.

The positive moment that had tried to come in vanished almost as quickly as it had appeared, and I succumbed to the black hole as Pete drew up alongside me. It was the only position we could be close together because of the traces and pulks behind us. The struggle finally got to me. It overwhelmed me. I became the struggle, and it all poured out.

"Pete, I'm much too slow. I'm hopeless at finding the right way. We'll never make it. All these extra miles they keep giving us are making it impossible. We'll never get there in time. I don't like the cold. I just want to be home and safe."

Drops of liquid heat touched my cheeks, froze like a stream of diamonds and clattered into icy hard goggles tempered only by the soft wind of a heavy sigh. The sensation touched me at a deep level as more heat filled my eyes.

"Come here," Pete said.

Strong arms reached out and lovingly enfolded me. At last I felt safe. It made me cry more and I sobbed uncontrollably. Finally I let go. All that holding on so tight for so many months. All that fear that had been chasing me, asleep and awake, biting at my heels, laughing at me for brandishing my sword of bravery. Although I had kept on running and hadn't dared turn and face it as I did now, plunging the sword deep into its heart, not caring that the sword was made of china, not steel, and to use it caused it to shatter into a thousand pieces.

I felt like I was left with no shell, no armour and with nothing to defend myself. Just open empty space, a new sensation akin to freedom.

We had stayed too long. I was beginning to shiver. "C'mon," said Pete in a tone that revealed how worried he was about me. "We're getting cold. We're not 21 any more, are we? I'll lead for a bit."

I followed gratefully. Although still close to the edge of tears, I felt comforted by angelic hugs and also remembering that Rowena at the White Eagle Lodge had seen many shining beings of light accompanying me, but the tough conditions continued. We pushed on into the late afternoon and the sastrugi became larger still, making it harder to weave in between without visibility. The wind picked up, so we felt even colder. I was reduced to running on the skis with short quick steps behind Pete to try and stay warm. Then, wrestling with a particularly awkward piece of sastrugi, I fell over and then did the same again. Pete fell too. I tried to haul him up but couldn't and ended up down again in a heap. It was difficult with skis and pulks and sticks pulling in all directions. After he had fallen again, we decided that rather than continue the Laurel and Hardy show we would make camp and put some weight back on the "plus" side of the "on the edge" scales. We would make up the bit of shortfall in our distance with a longer day and faster movement tomorrow. Please, dear weather angels, I prayed, could we have some sun tomorrow.

We had just put the tent up and lit a stove inside for that wonderful moment of warmth when we heard a vehicle. The wind had been making vehicle noises for days so I took no notice, but then we thought we'd better check. It was Alexis, Keith and Wolfman just passing by. Wow! It was more than good to see them. We waved for them to come over and they hovered, chatting for a couple of minutes before they froze. Yes, everyone's safely through the checkpoint and taking their own new line and yes, we'd made a good bearing. Suddenly I didn't feel so isolated and hard-done-by. My worries had just been irrational overflow.

A few minutes later the second vehicle appeared, for they always travelled in twos. Deirdre jumped out and rushed over to see if we were okay. She gave me a big motherly hug and I poured out how low I'd been feeling, thinking we were so slow and would never get there in the time. "Oh don't worry, we can always shunt you along a bit," she said so compassionately that I felt like crying again, but I understood that yes, sometimes in the world those that fall behind need to be picked up and shunted along, because everyone has to get there in the end, together.

We settled down to vegetable casserole with floating lumps of cheese followed by berries and custard, and the world felt a better place to be in.

It wasn't until I was in my sleeping bag and pulling my

resolute hat down over my eyes – thinking, please no more horrendous days like this one – when I suddenly realised there hadn't been an insight today. Then I understood. Of course. There hadn't been an insight because I hadn't been listening.

Ah...

"The struggle holds the pearl."

Thanks. Goodnight.

I might not have slept so well if I'd known we were about to have a reminder of the most hazardous and dangerous thing that can happen.

Warm Heart

I opened my eyes and there was warmth. The sun was out, the wondrous, all pervading, far-reaching sun. How totally lovely. It went straight through to my heart. Even the dreaded poo trip was almost bearable, well bare-able anyway.

"All is shining again," I said to Pete as I came back into the tent, wanting to share the joy.

He was beginning the water preparation. The stoves were his babies. After years of experience with different types he knew how to start them when they refused, coax them when they were sluggish and play with them when they were out of sorts. He liked working with these MSRs as much as I disliked it. In his usual meticulous way he brushed the ice off the two stove boards, each with its fuel bottle connected to a stove. We had found his board design a good way to be able to pack them away safely and be efficient, stable and readily available for use. He pumped each bottle 30 times to build the fuel pressure. Then with the first one, released the fuel tap on the bottle for three seconds, watching as a little petrol spilled into the stove dish and lit it with a match. Usually it is a matter of waiting for the yellow flame to reduce and turning the fuel tap on fully to catch a strong blue flame. This burns noisily, but is powerful enough to bring the heat needed for melting snow.

Today was different. There was a "phwham" sound. Without any warning the stove board lit up like a Christmas pudding as a wall of yellow flame shot up in front of Pete's face like a flash of sheet lightning licking the roof of the tent. Then a smell of burning nylon. I watched, horrified, holding my breath. Without even taking time to swear and with great presence of mind, Pete grabbed the flasks which, luckily, were still full and doused the flames. I breathed. Phew.

Somehow, fuel must have leaked during the night when the stove went out. What a lucky escape. Thank goodness the inner tent hadn't been damaged; a couple of seconds more and we might have had huge holes, or worse. It was all too obvious how crucial our protection was. The same thing had happened to the guys from Danske Bank on the acclimatisation trek. Everyone knew that it was a really good idea to not burn down the tent.

We let the stove board cool off outside and Pete managed to sew back the main floor tape of the tent. Normality returned. We were only a little late in setting off.

How good it was to be able to see where we were going. The landscape had been transformed by the sun. There was not a cloud in the sky. All was white again. Glistening lights and sparkles were everywhere. It was as though we sailed across a never-ending ocean abundant with frolicking sea horses, mighty whales coursing and pods of friendly dolphins darting and diving in pure delight. We joined in, shouting at each other the names of plates of food that we fancied:

"Bananas, of course - and scrambled eggs!"

"Chips!"

"Baked potatoes and salad!"

"Bacon and eggs!" It seemed that Pete had turned carnivorous. Must be the lack of oxygen to the brain. In any case, we had to stop the exquisite take-away orders; it made us too hungry. At the next lunchbreak, which was almost warm enough for our hands not to go numb but not quite, we had to make do with day-food and a handful of nuts and frozen cheese.

It wasn't long before Pete's exhaustion set in, so we took it slowly and steadily. He knew that if his body was responding as it normally did at sea level, he would be rushing ahead and I would be having trouble keeping up. It was intensely frustrating for him.

However, this speed gave me the opportunity to have gentle meditation time. As I was reaching the place in my mind where I go through my healing list of family and friends, an insight came through:

"Remember to send unconditional love to yourself."

Hmmm. I'd never thought of that. Although strange at first, I found this was a positive, energising thing to do. It was still on my mind when we stopped and made camp. Once we and all the gear were inside the tent, Pete bravely started with the stoves. This was the time for me to do the front porch jobs, as far away as possible at the other end. I collected all the water bottles and flasks from the day-sacks and replaced the day-food and chocolate for tomorrow. Then I swept out all the snow and ice that had collected in the inner tent and degombled the boots and gaiters before bringing them in. It generally took a couple of hours for the goggles and face masks to de-ice before we were able to start drying them. I had just broken off the worst of the icicles and was hanging them near the air vent when a vehicle drew up. The smiling face of Kenny appeared at the door.

"We want to move you forward again," he said kindly. "It looks like we're stuck with the new route round the U.S. exclusion zone, which means a lot of extra miles. So we'll position you within eight days of striking distance of the Pole." Our faces must have looked aghast because he added, "We know that with the planned time you would've done it."

"Thanks, Kenny." It was not easy for the race organisers.

So, that was it then. The universe had conspired again for it to be this way. I surrounded myself in a bubble of unconditional love. This helped me keep Egbert the ego under lock and key. There wasn't time to ski the whole distance. I had to accept it. Though I wasn't looking forward to going in that vehicle again.

Pete, though, was having a tough time. He appeared to be going through a similar sort of a fight that I had previously had with Egbert. He was annoyed with his body for not working the way he wanted it to. He felt it was letting us down. He was cross with the world, and I felt I received the brunt of it. He was furious with me for planning to tell about the tent fire in the diary call. He thought it would reflect badly on him. That not only was he going slow, but he had made a mistake. I tried to tell him that wasn't so and he was doing brilliantly, but he wouldn't listen. He was giving me plenty of opportunity to practise unconditional love for us both. Great, just what I needed.

In the morning he woke up with a realisation:

"I think I finally have to accept that I'm 62."

I wanted to tell him that I loved him *as* he was, like the knights of old – strong and true – and having to look macho was irrelevant, but I couldn't find the words. I could see in him the painful process that I had been feeling in myself, of another piece of the hard shell of self, cracking and falling away.

I wondered how Captain Scott and his four companions, Oates, Evans, Wilson and Bower, had coped with facing themselves and each other. Scott certainly wrote that he felt he had let his team down. Most would dispute that. We can only deduce their agony, and imagine how it was for them. Four of them at a time were pulling one long, heavy sledge, and five crammed into a tiny tent with no inner tent or sewn-in groundsheet. There was the hour it took every night for their bodies to thaw out the reindeer skin sleeping bags, and the pemmican and biscuits they ate every day until they ran out, holed up 11 miles from a supply depot in a uniquely severe eight-day blizzard on the return journey. They suffered from scurvy, frostbite, gangrene, starvation and exhaustion. There was no kind back-up team to pick them up when they faltered. They just died.

Scott's shadow continued to accompany us. Many nights at the end of writing my diary the words of the final entry in his would come to me: "It seems a pity, but I do not think I can write more." And frequently, when I went out of the tent for the necessary bare-able, I would repeat the famous words of Captain Lawrence Oates, "I am just going outside and may be some time." For Oates, it had been to sacrifice himself for the sake of the team. He had gone outside to his death.

Today was 17th January. This was the day in 1912 the five of them reached the South Pole after two and a half months of walking, and were greeted by the sight of the Norwegian flag tied to part of a sledge, facing the disappointment of coming second in the race. Only now could I appreciate at a deep level Scott's words written in a letter to the public, "Had we lived there would have been a tale to tell of the hardihood, courage and endurance of my companions that would have stirred the heart of every Englishman."

I knew that it was also on 17th January, but in 1773 that Captain James Cook in his ship, the *Resolution,* was believed to have been the first to sail over the Antarctic Circle. He was met by impenetrable ice 120 kilometres from the coast. These were the days before anyone had ever set eyes on this great southern land.

Today, 17th January 2009, team Southern Lights was greeted by a stunning spectral scene, as though not from this planet; I had never seen anything like it in my 60 years of life on Earth. One half of the sky was taken up by the sun. We could stare straight at it through an ethereal blue haze. The large central orb was pure white with six main spears of shooting light, joined by countless little ones stretching out and out until meeting an enormous rainbow circle which reached from the land to the top of the sky. Like a buoyant translucent sphere, effortlessly balancing. From the edge of the halo more light stretched in all directions, enveloping the land and the sky in its aura.

It was cold, minus 43°C, the coldest we had experienced so far. There was a very strong wind, blowing mostly around our feet. In an endless sea that came from the far distant arc of the horizon beneath the sun, a mist of diamond dust rushed, swirled at our presence and passed on in an endless journey to the arc on the other side. It was as though a huge dragon had drawn breath and was blowing playfully across this little moon. Everything was a beautiful pale ice blue, from the snow to the mist to the sky. The only sound was a low whusssssssh as ice crystals jostled and danced with each other; the whole of the Antarctic appeared to be on the move. We could only stare in wonder and move in circles to instinctively maintain some warmth, but it felt right to be ice cold too, to be part of this magnificence.

If someone had said the end of the Earth is nigh, I would've understood it. Of course that was where we were heading anyway.

In all the ice cold, my heart was burning with the richness and wholeness of the experience. I was being touched by something too big to comprehend. It was the feeling from antiquity that the gods are looking after us. That all is well. That all is as it is meant to be. If I had wanted a sign, I could never have invented one so powerful. Everything was unfolding perfectly, a sense of a great gathering of energies ahead of an important happening. I knew that we were not meant to be pushing ourselves to the limit. Our energy was being saved for what was before us, that we should prepare well as we neared our goal. Trust that all would work out.

This was a day when we didn't need to be battling against the elements. It was too awesome.

The spell of the scene was broken as the support team picked us up. The vehicle travel wasn't as bad as I had anticipated. Sarah found me sea-sick pills and noodles.

The lift became two days and then three as the vehicles suffered multiple break-downs. Firstly it was a back axel. Kenny and Wolfman dug a workshop pit underneath a corner of the vehicle so they were protected from the wind, cut a bit off a trailer and welded, fixed and mended. One of the trailers was to be abandoned here with drums of fuel to be picked up on the return journey. The four vehicles were to be driven all the way back to Novo after reaching the Pole, covering a total mind-blowing distance of 5,000 kilometres. We set off in the truck called Bruce, which had temporarily lost its 4-wheel drive capacity. We were towed in a bucking bronco ride before the next problem hit. A bit of compressor-pipe had become stuck in the exhaust and melted. Wolfman had designed and created the special modifications for these extreme conditions. He was a mechanical wizard. He needed to be.

Meanwhile, we waited. We weren't the only ones. Petter and Martin were pacing up and down, frustrated at not being able to film Missing Link. Their boys were doing amazingly well. Once we were on the move again we were able to see how the race was progressing, as we were in the vehicle at sched-call time. Missing Link was still in the lead by a margin of 33 kilometres, but they were running out of food. QinetiQ was battling on in second place, but James was suffering bad feet. Close behind was Danske Bank, struggling with severe weather. Following them was Due South, concerned about the extra mileage they were having to do, and a little way back was South Pole Flag who were requesting a doctor; Simon had frostbite on one ear and three fingers. Sarah, working on the vehicle intercom, was able to contact Doc Ian in the car in front and speak with Tony on the satellite phone to pass on the coordinates of the teams. She spoke to André in the UK who was doing the website to pass on the positions. Finally, she plugged the satellite phone into the laptop and emailed him the up-to-date news and forwarded the day's photography. Office work done.

We were dropped off with our pulks restocked and only 130 kilometres to do via a dog-leg around the exclusion zone. As the vehicles bounded off in a cloud of snow, we noticed a handful of biscuits that had fallen from the closing door and rushed to scrape them from the snow. Every mouthful of sustenance was precious here. It had been good to be with the support team but wonderful to just be us again. We put our little red tent up and looked round at the 360° view of white to the horizon, decked with shining lights. Wow, how lovely, I sighed. Back in the heart of this beautiful land and all was well. It was still excruciatingly cold, but the wind had momentarily dropped. We fell asleep in the arms of Antarctica, rocked by complete and utter silence.

Conditions were still good in the morning, though as we set off I was aware that my toes were numb. Trust in the movement, I told myself, they'll come back. But I was interested in other things. I couldn't wait to return to my own mind journey, to replenish the inner fuel.

I went through my meditation routine and the insight was:
"Send warm heart unconditional love to everyone."

So I sent bubbles of warm heart unconditional love to all on my usual list, the racers and the support team and then to everyone in the world. It was like going round giving hugs of light.

"And send warm heart unconditional love to the Earth."

In a similar way, practising this was like giving a hug to the Earth. I saw it bathed in a pale pink light, the colour of rose quartz, the colour of love. I knew this should be the technique to use at the peace ceremony.

It made me feel positive and that together we can all help our struggling Earth to get back into balance. To go for peace on Earth. This means peace for the environment and all beings. And, of course, peace for humanity.

There's a calling...

Pulling for Peace

W"hy are you going so slowly?" Pete called from behind me.

I was pulling the weight of 10 days' supply of food in my pulk and the snow was very soft, but there was little sastrugi and I didn't think the pace was much different from the plodding we'd been doing all along. That could only mean one thing: Pete wasn't feeling exhausted. Clearly the rest days had put weight back on the "plus" side of the "on the edge" scales. It fact, it was the first time he could remember not feeling exhausted. Knowing his normal go-for-it approach, I could only marvel at what he had managed to work through to get this far. No doubt his soul was learning huge amounts about patience. All useful stuff for a knight.

We were following the vehicle tracks as they headed south on our route. This was particularly helpful when, after a while, the sun disappeared and a blanket of cloud came down. The bitter cold turned into sharp dagger cold. I was having trouble with my goggles misting up and freezing out any visibility. I found that if I could keep my hood off and occasionally lift my goggles into the wind there wasn't a problem, but right now a severe wind was blowing from the east and the left side of my face was iced up and numb. My nostrils were frozen. Sniffing had a strange crunchy note to it and my attempts at breathing through my nose were only achieved accompanied by a sort of whistle.

I felt sure that if I could see my face there would be white patches of frost-nip. This is an early, reversible stage of frostbite, before the flesh becomes waxy hard and deep frozen. So I wriggled my nose as hard as I could and scrunched my face repeatedly. The frostbite vulture can attack in as little as 30 seconds; he was not to be trifled with. The hood had to go up. These jacket hoods had fur ruffs. They came forward around the face, keeping the wind off and creating a little micro-climate within. Researchers had tried every type of material available but nothing worked as effectively as natural fur. The thought of this had greatly upset me at first, but after learning that it was the fur of sledge dogs that had died naturally – having enjoyed a life of crossing the ice – it didn't seem so bad. I just thanked the dog and appreciated the protection.

Once my hood was up, turning to check on Pete skiing behind became the problem. However, when the sun returned it was easy to just glance to the side to see his shadow. This worked up to about 4pm. After that the sun gave some warmth to the right side of the face anyway. The big thing was not to turn my face into the wind. As always, everything we did here was dictated by the wind.

Then, oh help. It occurred to me I had ignored any fundamental inner connection with that element. I thought I had better rectify this. I breathed deeply and tried to open the essence of my being to be at one with the essence of the being of the wind. "Wind, oh dear wind, I honour you and thank you for allowing us to be here. Please, stay calm for a few more days for us." I felt different after that. Not so much an interloper in this breath-taking world, but part of it. I had taken a crucial step of harmony with all that was around me. Why had I taken so long to undertake such an important courtesy to Brother Wind?

The insight came with a feeling of spaciousness and movement:

"The presence of fear blinds the knowing of oneness."

Of course. It had been the fear. I checked inwardly and

happily found no fear.

After that, even though the day seemed to go on forever, I was content, and there was an interesting effect to think about. I could swear that the horizon was nearer, indicating that we were going uphill. Pete insisted that it was flat. After my experience of trying to avoid going round in circles I thought I'd keep quiet. Maybe the perception was a result of always seeing the curve on the horizon, or of my being shorter than Pete, or of my notion that we were approaching the top of a mountain. Whatever, the fact remained that we often had differing perceptions on things.

We were two people close to each other in a relatively uncomplicated environment. What of the nearly seven billion citizens of the world? Even before taking into account things like almost one third are under the age of 15 or two thirds from Asia, that's a lot of differing perceptions to roll into one bundle of peace and harmony, but I felt excited that the members of the human family were now beginning to pull together to face the oneness of global issues, for a new world order. Today was 20th January, the day of the inauguration of the new U.S. president, Barack Obama.

It was intriguing too, to turn my thoughts to a system of being more in harmony with my body. I tried stopping when it felt like it was time to eat or drink. It seemed to work equally as well as struggling to find my watch to check the time and wasn't physically a lot different. Perhaps our skiing bodies were just ingrained with "stop for chocolate every hour, drink and day-food every two". Even so, I found I couldn't take in half of what I needed at these stops, or in the tent. That evening I struggled to finish the cinnamon rice pudding even though I had been really hungry all day.

Communication was never easy on the satellite phone. Tonight's stilted conversation with Sarah was no exception. We understood that we should hang back a bit for the other racers by cutting down our daily distance and not do the route that we were given yesterday but to continue to follow the vehicle tracks.

Egbert managed to force his head out. "Oi! I'm fed up with

all these changes. I feel like a pawn in someone else's game, and I've been cheated of the race challenge I came for."

"Egbert, go away!" I replied firmly, securely mending the lock that he had broken. "Our personal ego challenge is entirely irrelevant. We don't need it. We've done stuff like that before. It was never the intention. We are rising above it and concentrating on the mission ahead. It's the race for the Earth that's important. That's what we came for. We must move forward gently with a warm heart."

An insight confirmed this as we were skiing the next day: *"Know acceptance. Trust that all is perfectly unfolding."*

Okay, I will be accepting and I will trust. Especially with my hands. Today they seemed to be taking longer and longer to come back into circulation after breaks, and it was worrying that Pete had had no feeling in the tips of two of his fingers for a couple of days now. He was working on trust too. We could see on each other the ice that crept over us through the day, white, sticky and merciless – like a slime mould. It smothered the goggles and face masks, penetrated the balaclavas, the neck gaiters, the inside of the jackets, clung to the straggly bits of my hair and grew with delight over Pete's moustache and beard so he looked like he'd fallen into a tub of vanilla ice-cream. That was probably the one food we could live without at the moment.

Though we had visibility and no clouds, there was no bright sunlight and no dancing sparkling lights. I knew and trusted that they were there. Our world had been taken over by an ice blue that allowed little reflection but gave the snow a watery shimmer. A new type of peace pervaded. There was not a dolphin in sight, just a calm, flat sea. Even the sun, large and low throughout the day, seemed to freeze and meld into the sky, with no definition of where sun ended and sky begun.

We made camp after only six hours skiing to keep our distance down as requested. I felt like I hadn't done anything today; most days I felt like I'd run the marathon. Pete said it was frustratingly like the slow train waiting outside Waterloo for the express to come by. Even so, we both found it hard

214

to get stiff old bodies to bend down and remove the skis. He had managed to have exhaustion for only half of the day and then encouragingly complained about my speed as he was getting cold. I think, although we had adapted slowly to the intense cold, we had both lost a lot of weight and so were feeling it more, and the temperature seemed to be dropping daily (it was getting to the end of summer).

I looked out of the tent through the shelter of the door where the zip was down a bit at the top. A little patch of sunlight came through as it often did in the evening and was almost hot. How beautiful it felt on my face. I could just make out a faint halo around the sun. Everything felt in harmony. I had even been accompanied on my MP3 player today by a file called "gentle sounds" which had fitted perfectly with my mood. I felt drawn to pull out the little ninth citrine crystal from my heart pocket where I was keeping it safe. I held it up. It shone brilliantly, golden to the light, catching pieces of rainbow facets. Turning it in my fingers, I imagined I saw a waving curtain like the flare of a dancing aurora. There was a sense that a time of purpose was drawing near.

It was nearer than we realised. Tonight's conversation with Sarah brought more changes:

"We have permission for the remaining racers to cross the exclusion zone. This means that you can now go due south and come straight to the Pole. Take two days and camp at 15 kilometres."

"So who's made it already? Who's won?"

She wouldn't tell me.

We checked on our GPS. It was 29.7 kilometres to S89 59.999. It wasn't able to record S90. That was the end of the Earth.

Wow! The shock of only two days to go set my mind reeling. Now I could see the end. The goal that had been so far in the future for so long, suddenly is almost upon us. I don't feel ready. It's what I've wanted for so long, dreamed, planned, yearned, trained, fundraised, pushed myself mentally and physically, all that effort. Suddenly it's almost here. I can't get my head around it. I need to prepare mentally. It'll mean only two more days of my meditations. My insight training, I'm not ready to stop that. I want there to be more days. I've still no idea how the peace ceremony will work. We can't mess up the main purpose. When should we activate the crystals? When should we put them in their final resting place? Where and how? What about the timing for the ceremony? We always assumed we'd be arriving at the last minute. Now we're bound to fly out too early and we won't have 29th January at the Pole. Everything will be out of kilter for those tuning-in with us. Oh help.

"Calm down," said Pete, watching me with a big grin on his face. "Hey, in two days time we'll be at the South Pole."

"Yeah," I smiled, remembering all is unfolding perfectly. "I can't wait to be there. To the South Pole and beyond!"

Amazingly, there was a part of me that was still not sure. For weeks now I'd been thinking never ever, *ever* again, but now there was something in me that wanted to keep going, even... even... do it again, perhaps. Forget it! No way! Crazy! Where did that thought come from? It went rapidly, tail between its legs.

I awoke in the morning feeling completely drained. The short day yesterday had meant an early meal. Pete had been waking up through the night because of his breathing difficulties and having midnight chocolate feasts; I hadn't eaten for 12 hours. There was nothing left in my tank. I felt floppy, dehydrated and wobbly. It was all too easy to forget the basic rules of fuelling the body. I sat up in my sleeping bag and the thought of reaching the South Pole hit me. It stuck in my throat. My eyes filled with tears and my chin quivered. I sighed heavily, trying to stop the surging emotion in my chest. The end of all that effort was just too much. Knight-in-shining-armour to the rescue with a hug.

"To the South Pole and beyond!" he encouraged.

"Perhaps we could leave the beyond for the moment," I sniffled pathetically.

"Have another hour's sleep."

I looked at his familiar face etched with the weariness of such a long struggle. I saw the gentleness and the strength that I loved and through the kindly eyes I saw compassion. This touched my heart in its open and vulnerable state and I allowed the tears to fall.

I curled up in my sleeping bag, but didn't go back to sleep. Instead, I imagined myself receiving a healing at the White Eagle Lodge. Getting up for the second time, I felt better and headed out happily into the day.

Conditions were the same as yesterday. We were held in a pale, peaceful ice blue world. The enormous halo of the sun, cloud-like with barely a suggestion of any colour, was more pronounced today and gave me the perception that it was guarding us on our way. How I loved this beautiful wilderness. I felt part of the land, the snow and ice, the Earth, the wind and the sky. It was as though my heart resonated with the same rhythm. I was the wildness and the beauty, the rawness and the purity. Every cell in my body was with it in harmony. Things were how they were meant to be. Timeless and forever. I never wanted it to end, but I knew too that I was the end, as I was the beginning. I could never ask for anything more for I was everything.

This beautiful feeling of oneness allowed an insight to drift in:

"Peace comes from a calm, loving and pure energy."

I saw then, without a doubt, that we should do the crystal activation ceremony tonight, here in this purity, before reaching what was bound to be a busy energy at the South Pole. So the lead-in was now. Perfectly in tune, my little MP3 machine played out all the Peace Messages. They were coming to their rightful home, bringing dedication, love, caring, joy and hope from representatives of humanity. I was reminded then of life's priorities.

Pete and I discovered that each of us had a list of all the things that we longed to do on returning home. The things that had brought a lump to the throat in the toughest times and helped carry us through long, cold hours. That afternoon we spent a happy time sharing them.

"Taking my kids skiing," he started.

"Skiing with my brother, definitely downhill," I responded.

"Building a shed in my garden."

"Going to the theatre with Marco and Chloe."

As well as the times with my sons and their partners, there were the chats with my Mum and sisters and the preciousness of being there to see my little granddaughter, Elsie, grow up. To hold her hand, see joy on her face, listen to her giggles, and for good measure I thought I'd chuck in birdsong, some luscious green plants, or any green plants, and maybe the smell of freshly baked bread, let's keep it simple – anything hot would do. Did I need to walk to the South Pole to appreciate how important these things are?

Despite, Pete's exhaustion and a backache that he had developed, we made a good pace. The ice was flat and smooth. The pulk I pulled behind me felt light. I thought of all the times that I had struggled with the heaviness holding me back and throwing me off course. My little sky dancer was now as much a part of me as I was of it. Like my mind and body, we were now in tune, but by the afternoon the effort in the pulling motion had made me hot. It was a hot day. The still-air temperature had risen to minus 26°C, the hottest we had experienced for some time. A gentle wind was bringing the wind chill down to only minus 37°C. Almost tropical.

I began to sweat, but didn't do anything about it as we had just about reached our distance for the day. Unfortunately, we had strayed off last night's longitude. I didn't think this made any difference. Pete decided that we should get back onto the exact line as a good navigation exercise. We turned into the wind on what seemed to me to be a backtrack arc. I soon became really chilled, and after an hour my patience had worn thin. I became annoyed.

"I don't want to go to the *North* Pole," I shouted crossly.

I grumpily sent a bubble of unconditional love and then smiled to myself as it made me feel better. Ah, a little test to check that I'm holding the energy needed. Thanks, universe, it really wasn't necessary. The test had come anyway. I realised that I didn't have to be feeling loving to send unconditional love, but I did need to be mindful and find ways of changing grumpiness to lovingness for life to flow well.

By the time the tent was erected on the exact longitude, I had a satisfied knight, though I was frozen through so much my hands had gone numb. For the first time, it took a while to get the stoves going. When that moment of heat came we appreciated it all the more, and we were warm for the diary call. We left the message for everyone that we were starting the peace ceremony process with the crystal activation tonight, adding that the more people that were able to tune-in with us at 9pm for the next few days, holding thoughts for the peace and harmony of our Earth, the more powerful it would be.

Just before 9pm, we donned duvet jackets, grabbed the sacred bag and headed outside. I marvelled at the ethereal light. The sun, muzzy but bright, stood guard to the southwest. A tall pillar of light reached up to it from the Antarctic ice within the huge halo that filled up the sky. There was the slightest hint of rainbow colours in it, otherwise all was still bathed in a hazy pale ice blue, smooth and flat from horizon to horizon. There was a complete pure spaciousness, as though our feet were standing on nothing. All was calm. All was peaceful.

We took a few steps from the tent to a patch of snow perfectly polished by the wind. Here we took the shovel and carved the figure of a six-pointed star expressing complete harmony. Within it, we drew a circle. I breathed deeply at the beauty and wonder of the moment, allowing the vibration to rise. I pictured in my mind a bubble of light holding the Earth and filled it with warm heart unconditional love, drenching it in rose quartz pink, and spoke out:

"We have carried these crystals across the Antarctic to be the facilitators to send off the Peace Messages from the end of the Earth and uphold the Climb For Tibet star of peace. We now call to start the activation process."

Pete and I hugged. Kneeling, I took the crystals from the bag. In the Tibetan style of showing respect I touched each crystal to my forehead. Then I placed the nine citrines around the circle with the double-ended quartz shift crystal to the south and the rose quartz in the centre. I was transported in my mind to a golden spiral rising higher and higher, my head buzzing and lifting. I longed to continue but knew I must stay grounded. Together we chanted "OM" and the vibration of the sound of the universe resonated from this place of purity and peace out and across the cold and beautiful Earth. The crystals glowed and shone magically. The sense of presence was strong. The presence of awakening.

Our little ceremony was awesome.

We had great anticipation for tomorrow.

When we woke up, the tent was warm from the sun. I poked my head through the door zip. We had a shining white world. The visibility was great.

"Hey, Pete," I called excitedly, "come and look. Quick. I can see something on the horizon."

The End

Could just a tiny blip be the end of the Earth?
"No that's not anything," said Pete. "Anyway, it can't
be the South Pole. It's in the wrong direction. Look, the
compass points south about 25° to the right." I checked it
out on the GPS, which involved taking a moving reading by
walking a few paces. Yes, allowing for the compass deviation
of 2° it indicated the same direction. I stared at the little
yellow machine in the palm of my gloved hand. It was on
the end of a ribbon around my neck, so that I could shove
it down my front to keep the batteries warm and be readily
available, along with my camera, compass and MP3. My
pulse quickened to see the distance it showed at the top of the
screen. Only 14.6 kilometres.

Packing the pulks for the last pull, I attached our small
Tibetan flag to a flag pole that I had found conveniently
dropped by one of the others near the beginning of the race. I
fixed it on the back of Khandro, my Tibetan sky dancer, who
had shown so much service. The flag fluttered in the light
breeze. Now we would arrive flying the spirit of peace. The
other two Tibetan flags on the pulk-covers were still intact
although battered, as was Elsie's Peace Message now faded to
a beautiful memory. The words written on the pulk had long
since rubbed off, battered by storm winds and blizzards, their
essence left along the trail as messages of hope, and proudly
pulling, as the figurehead at the prow of the pulk, was Gaius.

He was now battle-worn and bent horizontal in a defiant, racing-penguin position. His toes and beak were frost-bitten and tattered. Gone was his youthful, sleek appearance, replaced by an ice-covered wrinkled coat. Ah, but he had tales to tell of hardihood, courage and endurance that would stir the heart of every penguin.

We set off and because the snow was so flat and smooth we skied together side by side for the whole distance. How nice it was to be able to share the eagerness of the day and communicate. After an hour there were two blips on the horizon where I had seen the mirage earlier. One was long and dark and one faintly grey. We discussed whether they could possibly be the U.S. research station at the Pole but they still bore no connection to the direction south in which we were moving.

This was puzzling. Certainly images can become distorted under conditions of large temperature differences. Also, we knew from our climb of Chimborazo at the equator that – due to its spinning – our globe is not actually round but is an oblate spheroid. This means that it bulges at the equator and is flattened at the poles, so our horizon was not quite so curved here. I looked around. Yup, it was correct. Things looked pretty flat. Perhaps it was even more so because of the weight of the ice deforming the shape of the Earth here too. But no matter how hard I tried, these thoughts didn't help to explain the fact that if the blips turned out to be the South Pole then we were heading somewhat in the wrong direction to reach it. Maybe some things are better left unexplained.

Things were simpler when I turned and looked behind us, past the pulks and the little flag. Apart from faint ripples in the ice we could have been on a milky glass lake. The only evidence of anything different was the two sets of tracks with round ski-stick marks dotted alongside, leading back to the horizon beneath the sun. This gave an emotive sense of the path that we had travelled together. The sun was emitting dynamic spears of light, accompanied by wisps of shiny high cloud, and shone so brilliantly it was throwing sparkles into the dazzling whiteness. No need of a halo today. It was hot again, still only minus 37°C, and the wind was the lightest we'd had for two weeks. An ideal day to arrive at the end of a planet.

At the first lunchbreak I removed my jacket, enjoying the sense of freedom that entailed and strapped it onto my pulk. As I did so, I noticed the patchiness of the colour. Under the arms were still a deep magenta, but most of the rest of it had faded, transformed by the sun into a beautiful rose quartz pink. Hmm. Was there a conspiracy going on? This oneness stuff seemed to work on many magical levels. And why was there a pink rose quartz coloured cloud hanging over the end of the Earth? We had set off more than a month ago to cross the Antarctic and not once had I seen a pink cloud. So what was this one doing here? Maybe all things always do work together, but I'm not often aware of it.

I felt grateful and honoured to have been a tiny part of this sacred wilderness, harsh as it was. I was happy. I didn't want it to end, but I wasn't prepared for the wrench that was about to come. It started with the sight of a vapour trail in the sky. I recoiled at its unnaturalness. How could man produce something so out of place, so civilised? The fact that my journey back to civilisation was to be by plane didn't matter. At the moment there was something in me that wanted to stay at home right here where I was.

As the day wore on, our route took us in a large arc around back towards the mirages. They had to be the U.S. base. Gradually we could make out a long black rectangle, round white domes and low brown and red shapes. It seemed to be a very sprawling mess of buildings. Though it felt like we could reach out and touch them, they took forever to come closer. It was exciting. We were reaching our goal. Yet at the same time it was uncomfortable and surreal that all this approaching ugliness could be it. As though coming to the outskirts of a city, we passed marker flags in the ice and skied underneath a cable. Then a large disk and a robot-looking contraption on stilts, behind which were laid out containers like at a seaport. Worst of all, behind a large building were four chimneys, belching grey smoke.

There was no sign of any people; it was empty and soulless. The inappropriateness clutched at my heart. It defiled the beautiful wilderness. Of course I'd known there was a base here and that polar research is vital to improve the understanding of our climate and environment, but somehow I'd always imagined it in the same romantic way that Amundsen and Scott would have found it. How can I have wanted something so much for so long and then not even like it when it came?

It's what it represents that counts, I told myself. It's not every day you walk up to the South Pole. Where should we be? Where *was* the South Pole? We followed the GPS direction through the base. The only sign of life was a large-wheeled people-carrier that drove near us and turned back. Then Pete pointed ahead. A few hundred metres away was a collection of round, orange people. Ah, that must be us. Suddenly, all the reasons for being here took hold. This was the end of the Earth. This was why we had worked so hard for so long. We had our important peace work to carry out. In the meantime, it was the end of the race. We would catch up with the others. This was where all the supreme physical effort could stop.

Two of the round, duvet-clad oranges came towards us. Approaching, we saw to our delight that it was Rune and Stian. As we hugged them, we noticed that underneath scraggly beards their faces were scabbed with frostbite and were gaunt and thin. They must have been through a great battle.

"Did you make it in first?" we asked.

"Yeah, we did it."

"Well done! That's so fantastic! Amundsen would be proud of you."

So it was Norway again. They had worked so hard for it, using all their skills of survival, and they had won. What a brilliant achievement. They led us via a circuitous route up a snowy mound to a large circle of flags within which a group of duvet-clad oranges had gathered, cheering and waving and holding cameras. And there it was. A red and white barber's pole with a shiny reflective ball on top. The ceremonial South Pole.

I turned my head to Pete and saw the warm gold of his jacket and the light brightly catching the goggles on the top of his head. Icicles were dripping from his mask onto the ice, which was caked white all over his face, but his eyes were shining.

"I shall probably cry," he said.

Was this my knight, with armour broken into a thousand pieces, shining from his inner self, my strong and true knight that I loved?

"C'mon," I said, grabbing his hand and raising our arms high as with the final effort we dragged the pulks up the little slope to the Pole, touched it together, turned and wound our arms around each other. Our eyes filled up. The tears fell warm onto our frozen cheeks. This was the end. This really was the end. We were caught up in the melee of racers, organisers and film crew swamping us with hugs and congratulations. It was a lovely welcome. Then somehow I had raised my head and was speaking to a camera rolling:

"We've carried Peace Messages from many hearts, with great effort and love, on behalf of our Earth," I proclaimed, the words quivering with emotion. "So this is for my little granddaughter," my voice cracked and I struggled to continue, "and for all the children of the world, that there may be a future of peace and harmony for them." And I broke down in wracking sobs.

Pete's announcement to the camera was emphatic and straightforward. "I'm never ever going near a pulk again."

We would see.

It was just after 5:30pm on 23rd January 2009. Team Southern Lights had skied almost 483 kilometres (300 miles) and now stood at the South Pole.

Or maybe not.

"Follow me," said Tony.

He was beaming, no doubt pleased that he'd managed not to lose his pensioners along the way. He led us across 50 metres of hard, trampled snow to an area set apart from the mound, to the geographic South Pole. Ah, the ceremonial Pole wasn't actually the southernmost point on the surface of the planet. At last we stood at the correct spot. Here, there was a small brass globe on a metal stake. This was where the Earth's axis of rotation hit the surface, the pivotal point around which everything was spinning. The problem was that because we were on an ice-sheet ever moving towards the sea at about 10 metres a year, this point was hard to catch. The marker was repositioned every year with a new brass design on 1st January, so we weren't far out of date.

We faced a large commemorative plaque. Under a little map of the Antarctic were two quotes. One, dated 14th December 1911 was by Roald Amundsen: "So we arrived and were able to plant our flag at the geographical South Pole." The other dated 17th January 1912 was by Robert F. Scott: "The Pole. Yes, but under very different circumstances from those expected."

I could relate to both their comments. They were both fine men, heroes of their time. Perhaps even more so, knowing Amundsen's words on learning about the tragedy of Scott and his companions: "Their deaths are more triumphant than most of our lives. Captain Scott left a record for honesty, for sincerity, for bravery, for everything that makes a man, and this to me is greater than even having discovered the Pole." Amundsen knew a thing or two about knights who were strong and true.

As we headed for the green mess tent, Pete heaved an immense sigh of relief and said, "Well, that's that then." I was pleased he didn't have a pen or I'm sure he would have been ticking South Pole off his list and planning what to do next.

In a wonderful show of caring, the boys had put up our tent for us and made hot chocolate. Not only were Stian and Rune here, but also Ben, Ed and James. They had come in yesterday 18 hours behind the Norwegians. It had been an epic and inspirational achievement to have come second, considering their lack of experience and having to manage the filming along the way. They had pushed themselves to the limit, with little sleep, and were now creeping around totally shattered with ulcerated feet, James through pneumonia and frostbitten fingers, and Ben a frostbitten nose. They had lost over two stone in weight each. Pete and I had lost one stone each. Our experience had been different because of the senior handicap, but we had also been severely tested. I even felt a bit guilty that whilst all the youngsters were in such a wrecked state, the little old granny had sauntered into the South Pole without even a jacket on, feeling great and with no frostbite. No doubt old-age caution and nutritional supplements had played their part.

But we still had work to do. It looked likely that we would fly out on the 28th. So we could not have the main Peace Message ceremony on the planned 29th. I put out a diary call explaining that the ceremony would now be on 26th January at 9pm, for people to tune-in with us. Sarah kindly put it on the website and we were pleased that Tony emailed the U.S. base with the details, too. We would tune-in for peace at 9pm every day anyway, knowing that many were joining us, including Ivy's anchor group in London and the eight support crystal holders. The last tune-in would be on the 29th. Sadly, it looked impossible to be with the main crystals then as, of course, we had to leave them here somewhere.

At the 9pm tune-in time I went out behind the tent and laid out the crystals again with a little meditation and an "OM". It was hard to concentrate being at the base with its weird noises like vehicles and strange banging, and the wind was getting up, whistling and whooshing through all the man-made constructions. I missed the silence of the wilderness.

By the morning, conditions had changed completely. As though the weather angels had been waiting for us to arrive, there was a massive temperature drop by 10°C to more than minus 46°C. The wind was still rising. We were so pleased not to be skiing, but three of the teams still were.

Christian, Gary and Gaz had predicted arriving at midday. It wasn't until 5pm that there was a call of "400 metres!" and we all grabbed orange duvets to rush out of our tents to greet them. My camera, which had lived round my neck, decided at this moment to run out of battery power. Amazingly it had survived on only two batteries since Novo and I had taken 1,500 pictures. Now I hurriedly pulled out a new battery that I had kept warm in a thermal pocket. It lasted only three minutes in this extreme cold.

I felt just as emotional seeing them come up to the ceremonial Pole as we ourselves were yesterday. There was a strong bond amongst the racers. We all cheered, clapped and hugged and said how proud we were of them. Three fine handsome men had set off. Three little old men arrived, with frostbitten faces, raw burnt lips and lifeless, ice-encrusted eyes.

Between us all we pulled their pulks to the tent area, erected theirs and melted copious amounts of snow for drinks for them. Gary had the energy to eat a meal we found for him. Christian and Gaz collapsed into their sleeping bags.

"I shall never complain about anything again," Gaz said.

Perhaps more people should walk to the South Pole.

It looked like it would take all the guys months to recover. Certainly I felt that if we had had to push ourselves similarly, the recovery time at our age would be even greater. However, I felt that somehow on the wider level we had been protected and looked after, so our energy was saved for the important job. We were a little part in a big operation for peace and the raising of consciousness. I resolved I would not fail.

The next day the weather deteriorated further. It was colder still and the wind was wilder. It was picking up snow as though it were nothing, throwing it here and there and relocating it in huge drifts. Visibility had gone and even the long dark base building, only 200 metres away, had no defined edges, blending in with the grey of the ice and sky. It was our turn to have an official tour of this, the Amundsen-Scott South Pole Station. It was newly erected as the old one had been nearly buried. We could see half of the old dome sticking out of the snow drifts. The new one was state-of-the-art and was designed on columns which could be jacked up and added to in separate pods as the snow level rose. They were rounded to reduce the drifts, which caused most of the problems.

The visit promised to be interesting. We entered through large double fridge doors, and there was the first fascinating item – heat. Wow! A lady greeted us with "You're all rather

fragrant aren't you." Which presumably is American for
"You stink." Well, we did have a shower six weeks ago. She
directed us to the second fascinating item – a washroom
with loos, mirrors and water that came out of taps. Double
wow, though little time to appreciate them. Things became
more and more surreal. It was like stepping into a James
Bond movie with long corridors, secretive research and a
big-brother-is-watching-you atmosphere. Although we were
really interested in the promised canteen visit with biscuits,
we had to go through a lot of other stuff first.

There was a strange official welcome. We were told in nice
friendly terms that they were fed up with tourists visiting
and interrupting their research programme. Apparently, there
had been quite a few groups lately. We were told that we had
to stick to rules and regulations and on no account could
any of their personnel be involved in a peace ceremony and
certainly no burning of Peace Messages was allowed. Right.
Understood, though I felt uncomfortable. We learned there
was even an order for all personnel to avoid fraternising with
the tourists. Obviously there were bureaucratic directives to
stick to. I suppose it was the same anywhere in the world,
but it was hard to be faced with it here. Pete asked Tony if
he would see if they would at least accept the written copies
of the Peace Messages after we had spoken them out. It was
really important to us to leave them here somewhere at the
South Pole, if possible, but it didn't sound hopeful, in view of
the official attitude.

We were then shown round. The principal scientific
programme, known as IceCube, was quite amazing. Buried
2,500 metres down in the pure and clear medium of this ice,
is the world's largest sub-atomic particle neutrino detector.
Neutrinos come from exploding stars and cosmic collisions.
The light created by their interactions is observed by
dropping photo detectors down holes cut by high-pressure
hot water into the ice. The members of the programme are
researching astrophysical phenomena such as the presence of
dark matter, basicly invisible stuff of the universe. No wonder
they didn't want us poking about.

Cold Hands, Warm Heart

We were told that about 240 personnel work here, of which 40 spend the winter. They'd have to like darkness a lot to do that, isolated from March to September with nothing but the Southern Lights to bring any natural light. No planes can operate in such extreme temperatures. However, things wouldn't be all bad. We saw a gym, a library and an artificial-light vegetable growing room. In one of the corridors, we were whooshed past photographs of the base in winter lit up by waves of green curtains, edged with purple. Ah, proof. But then we knew.

Back out in the cold, I took the crystals to the geographic South Pole for the 9pm tune-in. I felt that I was being watched. I looked over my shoulder. There was a vehicle close by and I knew I could be seen from the base. I decided to go for it anyway. I knelt and laid the golden citrines and the shift crystal in a circle around the marker, knowing that I'd just laid them out around the world. Then I placed the rose quartz adjacent to the marker and lay the Peace Messages alongside. I held warm heart unconditional love and visualised the Earth drenched in rose quartz pink with gold around it. I allowed myself to be drenched in golden light in a spiral and chanted the "OM".

Nobody came and arrested me.

By morning, the wind had dropped enough for the Basler to fly in to pick up the first group – the camera crews, Missing Link and QinetiQ. Whilst they were loading the plane with camera kit and then removing some because it was too heavy, I chatted with the pilot. He'd just tried to have a couple of hours sleep in a tent. He wouldn't eat or drink so that he didn't have to go to the loo on the flight. He seemed very edgy.

"Winter's coming in and the temperature's right on the margin for flying. We can't go below this. It's minus 50°C. There's too much weight, too much wind and the visibility's not good enough. I just wanna get the hell outa here."

He was faced with an eight hour flight to Novo, with a refuelling stop at a camp where Kenny was with two of the vehicles on their long journey back, but it looked like Novo weather might be too bad, so he would have to go further and drop the guys off at Troll, the Norwegian base. Somehow he still had to get into Novo to collect a new gear box for Bruce, then he would come back and pick up the remaining four teams.

In spite of my wanting so badly to be with the crystals at 9pm on 29th January, I sensed his apprehension and entreated him, "Please, please come back quickly."

Visibility did seem particularly dull. I wondered if it was anything to do with the solar eclipse that we were on the edge of today. It added an auspicious feeling to my anticipation. Today was the 26th, Peace Message Day. The sky was beginning to clear by the time the plane lifted off, just ahead of excited shouts of, "Due South's coming in!"

Three little figures came gradually closer, plodding towards us. Each step seemed to be a superhuman effort. Rachel was wearing her duvet jacket and had only one stick, keeping her spare hand over her face, whether to protect frostbitten fingers or her cheeks, I wasn't sure. She and Phil had had flu. They were all on their last legs. Amongst the hugs and clamour of "well done", I could only admire their incredible effort and cry with them too. They surrounded the Pole together and Rachel produced the flag for her music charity for blind children that had given her so much strength. How wonderful to see what the human body can put itself through and endure.

Christian, Gaz and I put their tent up whilst they collapsed into the green mess tent, where Pete and Gary melted enormous amounts of water for drinks. We had never seen people so dehydrated. There was some semblance of warmth from an inefficient fuel stove in the centre. It reminded me of one we had seen in Tibet fuelled by yak dung.

Now, here in the Antarctic at the end of the Earth the wind-horses were ready. It was around 6pm when we hung up the prayer flags and laid out the crystals on a little yellow mat for the Peace Message reading. Wonderfully the others, though worn out and dog-tired, found the energy to join in. It was lovely to do it with those who had just given so much of themselves. In turn, we spoke out every Peace Message, every wish, hope, prayer and pledge that we had carried across the frozen wilderness with love for our Earth. It was a focus for peace and harmony. It was a cry from many hearts for us all to take responsibility and work together in the world with the intention of the greater good.

My own wish was:

May I never have to hear my Elsie say:

"Granny, what *is* a polar bear?"

Or "Granny, why do grown-ups fight?"

Or "Granny, why don't we give food to children who are hungry?"

I knew that by holding warmth in our hearts we can enjoy the race for the future of our Earth. I knew that each one of us can make a difference and do something positive, no matter how small.

I was filled with hope.

Sarah and Doc Ian came in to share the end and told us that South Pole Flag were on the horizon. So now, around 9pm, they joined us as we carried the Messages up the slope of the mound across to the ceremonial Pole. We were hit by amazing light. All the low cloud and gloom had gone. The sun dazzled, picking up the colours of the 12 Antarctic Treaty Nation flags as they flapped, representing the peoples of the world. We knelt and drew the star and the circle as the sacred alter and laid out the crystals in their formation of wholeness. Alongside, we placed the Peace Messages which had been lovingly written by so many in the spirit of trust for a peaceful and harmonious Earth.

Then with open arms we offered them onto the winds of the planet. The wind-horses gathered in herds of light and sped away to work their magic, taking blessings and happiness to all beings. We had to squint our eyes against the light which was as bright as the brightest conditions we had seen. The crystals reflected the light, glowing richly. I welcomed the joining of others across the world tuning-in with us and gently called upon a higher vibration. In a profound moment of silence, I visualised gold spiralling around us, then the Earth held in rose quartz surrounded by gold. We chanted an "OM". All was perfect.

It was done. Hugs all round.

"Antarctica has taught me the importance of giving more hugs," Doc Ian said. Sounded like useful medical research to me.

The timing was great. The ceremony was finished just as the three figures of South Pole Flag drew close and headed our way. The Warrior and Simon leading Mark came up to the Pole in style to the usual emotional welcome.

"I shall have to stop hugging all these men," Mark joked. He was the first blind person to walk to the South Pole, and he was obviously okay. What a remarkable success story, sight or no sight. He was an inspiration to us all. As was Simon, but differently. He had been advised on medical grounds to give up, but had refused to quit. Now he was in a bad way, in a daze with critical, frostbitten fingers. Doc Ian didn't know if it would be possible to save them. A couple of days ago handwarmers had been dropped along the way for the team to pick up. If Simon's hands had not frozen again there was a chance. The Warrior had managed to get them both here and still looked as though he was on his Sunday afternoon stroll. "Oh, there's nothing to it," he said, but then, he's Norwegian.

All the teams were safe. The Messages had been spoken. It was almost time to go home, secure in the knowledge that dreams can be fulfilled whatever your age or ability. You just have to dream them.

But I couldn't relax. There was the crucial last part of the peace process to accomplish. The final placing of the crystals, for them to remain at the end of the Earth as a beacon of light. Crystals amplify energy, so it was important to send them off in the right way. The base had a haywire energy with rules and regulations everywhere and secretive, closed-off separateness, like a microcosm of much of the world energy. How were we ever to find the right space?

Was all the stripping down of the hard shell of ourselves, and the insight training to be in a heightened vibration, now to have been in vain?

And Beyond

I am pure white wilderness. There is simplicity and oneness and all is light. The sun is calling...

I awoke with a start. Knowing. We have to go back out.

"Pete. Wake up. We have to go back out into the wilderness to do the crystals."

"No way. I'm not going. I'm still having trouble breathing."

"C'mon. We have to go. We can't do them near the base."

"It's crazy, Tess. You know it's minus 50°C. It's warm in my sleeping bag."

"It'll be fine. You won't have your pulk to pull."

We left a couple of hours later. Stepping from the tent, we were hit by a maelstrom of spindrift, pouring in from the east as a carpet of diamond dust. Whilst we'd slept the wind had been busy. Our pulks had completely disappeared, as had the bamboo tent pegs. We clipped into our skis and looked around. The buildings were a misty blur. There was not a soul about. The rest of the racers were no doubt in their sleeping bags and the U.S. base worked on New Zealand time so it was the middle of the night for them. Great, we didn't want to be spotted. Without official permission our journey was illicit. It felt like we were breaking human law, but totally in tune with the natural law of the Earth.

We skied out away from the base and into the wind, breathing more easily now. There was a huge sun shining brightly, with an enormous halo taking up the sky, ethereal and otherworldly. Visibility seemed to be clearer here, especially above the snow which was coming towards us low at a tremendous rate, but we had our faces well covered and made a good pace. It was great to be back on skis and feel the muscles warm to the old familiar movement of ski, stick, ski, stick, and to hear nothing but the sound of the wind. It felt strange without my sky dancer, but there was a lovely freedom in having nothing to pull. I felt like I could ski all day.

I was almost too excited to feel the cold. The thought of minus 50°C would have been very scary once, but having built up to it over the weeks, perhaps our bodies were more used to it. Though more likely it was our minds. We knew now to always show respect. More than anything else, thoughts of the cold were dominated by the overriding purpose of our journey, which was about to be fulfilled. This was the culmination of all the months of effort. This was the final part of our mission. I briefly went through my meditation routine and everything felt fine. All was perfect. All was ready.

We had been following the runway marked by large metal flags every few hundred metres. Now at last we moved beyond. Beyond the influence of humanity. This was the pure-air zone up wind from any pollution at the base. From here it was wilderness, raw, pure and white. I knew that our direction was to be taken from the sun. I took an angle towards it. It was calling me. There was no doubt in my mind whatsoever that this was the way and that the position of the sun was crucial. We moved directly towards it, stunned by the brilliance of the light. The halo stretched around the sky displaying a faint rainbow colouring. In the centre, the large dazzling orb shot six main spears out almost to the edge of it. On the lower side one came straight down to the ice, a shining spear of light.

I turned to Pete. "What do you think? Just beyond that little lump?"

"Perfect," he replied.

Although here near the Pole the sun is roughly at the same

height in the sky throughout a 24-hour day, the timing was such that it was at an apparent zenith point. Amazingly, it was the moment of the day when our shadows pointed due south, with a direct line from the sun through our spot south to the Pole. Yes, perfect.

We removed our skis and placed our day-sacks in the snow. Empie peered out of his pocket on mine, along with the fluttering prayer flags bringing colour and sacredness to the scene. Pete grabbed the shovel from his and started digging. He dug a metre square to a depth of about half a metre.

"A bit more this way," I said. "So they'll be in the sun."

He looked up from his work. "You only brought me along to dig the grave, didn't you."

"Yeah, and because of your compassionate heart," I replied with a smile.

He marked a little six-pointed star and a circle in the snow. I laid the crystals out in their now familiar formation, with the shift quartz to the south. Next to the rose quartz I placed the chip of all the Peace Messages, no bigger than my little fingernail. The citrines glowed brightly as I pictured the Earth in rose quartz and gold.

"Love you," we said to each other as we hugged.

Then spoke out into the wilderness, "Oh Divine Spirit, precious Earth, dear Antarctica and shining beings of light, we humbly offer these crystals for peace."

The ceremony was simple, but undertaken with great love. Our mission was done. The crystals had been returned to the Earth, from whence they had come, now programmed for a wider harmony.

"Let's go home," said Pete. "I've completed my part in getting you safely here."

He filled up the hole with snow – snow formed from brother ice crystals, each in their own six-pointed star formation – and we smoothed it over. Within an hour the wind would have scoured the surface, obliterating all trace of its existence along with our tracks. I looked longingly at the ruffled snow which indicated the spot, burning the image into my mind. Beyond it was smooth white wilderness blazing with light across to the horizon. Above it reaching up towards the sun, shone a new semi circle of light that hadn't been there before.

Our hands and faces had gone numb. Clipping into our skis, we headed back. We had come quite far. It wasn't possible to see the base except for the tiny faint outline of one of the large disks, so hopefully no one would have seen us. My goggles misted up and froze so I couldn't see anything anyway. I didn't mind. My heart was singing.

Once I had defrosted in the tent, I carefully put all the sheets of Peace Messages together with the children's originals into the sacred bag and took them to Tony.

"I'll find a way for them to stay at the base," he said. "Don't worry."

Tony was a hard, tough military machine, a man who dealt with things by chucking orders around. He had come up trumps again. Not only had he been the driving force to make the race happen, and safely, but he'd known what mattered to us more than anything, just like in the Arctic. There he had sacrificed his own journey to enable us to be on the plane to the magnetic North Pole and carry out our peace ceremony. To us, that had meant a great deal. I thought too of the time he had told us that his purpose in Iraq had been to bring peace to the region. Now, when we were despairing that we'd ever get through to the Americans with our Peace Messages, he was on the case. Behind all that gruff military manner was a heart of gold that cared about world peace.

"Have a look in that pulk over there," he said. "That's the last spare food in the camp."

I found a vegetarian dinner and some nuts. Pure gold.

We ate in the tent, longing for the times of abundant food, and listened to the sound of a rising wind. This turned into a booming, slashing blizzard. Everyone was low on food and just wanted to go home, but how was the plane going to land in this? And would the temperature stay above the critical minus 50°C?

The blizzard raged all night. By morning, it was weirdly dark in the tent. The entrance had been completely covered.

We had nearly been buried alive. Now I understood why we always kept one of the shovels inside.

"I'll leave the job of freeing us to you, so you can be the superhero," I said to Pete.

"As long as I can do it from my sleeping bag, I don't mind what it is," he replied and cleared a hole to reach through with the shovel, before going back to continue a 16 hour sleep.

Through much of the day and into the evening, I dozed and lay listening to the throbbing sounds of Antarctica's wild orchestra playing its heart out. The vibration touched me at the deep core of my being.

I am part of this wind. I am part of this wild purity and supreme force where man is so puny, so pathetic. We can struggle and pit ourselves against it for a while, but the wilderness always wins. It's too strong, too powerful for it to be any other way. And the base? Well, the base sits in its path, thinking it's in control, smoke belching from its chimneys, trying to reign with rules and causing imbalance, a disharmony. Only one rule can be king here. The rule of the Earth.

The natural harmony that cleanses, that balances, that freezes all, that dances round the sun in the sky sparkling with ice crystals, diamonds of this cold world that is sometimes shattered into rainbows, splitting the white into its component parts throwing colour over this deep white land and then gathers into formation and dances round the sun in supplication as sundogs, complete circles and pillars standing to attention. Sun, beautiful sun, who hangs supreme for six months only to disappear and leave trust, trust that all the systems will return, burning through the empty ozone layer to blaze again. The wind is not angry, but kind, for that is its nature. The cold is not fierce, but pure, for that is its nature. The emptiness is not severe, but free, for that is its nature. The snow is not overpowering, but beautiful, for that is its nature.

Oh shining ethereal Antarctica we will never forget that you allowed us here with such alacrity and the welcome of a thousand lights. Thank you for this privilege, this honour.

Cold Hands, Warm Heart

Cold as cold as ice can be with the warmth long to be held in our hearts. We shall tell others of your music and your natural systems fighting for survival in the only way that they know and man can help or hinder. He can flow together with respect or he can continue on the path of destruction, but there is hope. From open hearts and from the children of man, and other beings who are trying to help. Listen to the children, listen to their Peace Messages. They know, they know.

Wind keep blowing here and we will hear the Messages on some foreign shore where, as a warm breeze, you caress a palm tree grove and roll grains of sand into a gentle blue ocean or rustling wet through jungle foliage profound and richly verdant with life in a thousand circles or whipping cheerily down the main street of a city, picking up cast-off chip packets to dash against brick walls built to withstand your chills. It cannot be separated. Wind, there are no walls. This is one island, one being, one world. How can we draw boundaries and say "I will control"? It can only be temporary for there is no control, but for seconds of pretence.

Ah, you sigh, Brother Wind, you sigh for the sadness, but there are those hearts that care. I know. I know things are turning. There is great confusion and a commotion never known before in the systems of man. It is breaking down and making way for the new and you will blow across harmony. I swear you will. For it is the only way, and all other ways will pass into the mists of time. Dear wind, dear wind, we will try and listen and blow with you. I will try and hear your drum which beats in my heart now. I will try and carry it with me.

At this moment my outpouring paused. The booming quietened and stopped as though someone had turned off a tap. I unzipped the tent and looked outside. The wind had stilled. The time was exactly 9pm. How awesome.

Sarah had asked everyone to come out at this time to pose for photos with flags at the Pole.

"How incredibly lucky, the wind's stopped," she said.

Pete fixed the Tibetan flag to the sticks and we marched it proudly up to the Pole to place it briefly amongst the dozen Antarctic Treaty Nation flags. These were the original nations who signed the treaty in 1959. Today, there are 47 countries. Yes, we were indeed honouring their priorities of nature, peace and science.

As we finished the last photo and headed back, the wind picked up again, though without its previous severity. "Thank you for your sensitivity, Brother Wind," I whispered. I had a profound feeling that all the elements were on my side. It took me back to some time of long, long ago with the deepest understanding that I had ever remembered. It was more than a time of knowing, it was a time of simply being Earth. I felt that this memory was a precious gift from the Earth in exchange for our gift of healing crystals powered with Peace Messages from those who care. I remembered how fearful I had been before the start of the race and now I was leaving in a state of love and oneness. Thank you, dear Earth. May I honour and do justice to this gift.

There was no more than a stiff breeze when, at 10:30 the following morning, the sound we'd all been waiting for came. First just a vibration, then a distant buzz and finally the roar of the engines of the Basler circulating overhead, landing and taxiing across the open area of the base to a halt near the tents.

Not surprisingly, the pilot was worn out and instead of flying straight back had requested a tent to sleep in. We were told to be ready to take off at 7pm. Today was the 29th. So it looked like our final 9pm tune-in was to be in the air. Ah well, lots of room for higher thoughts.

When there was no action by 7pm I went to check with Tony. He was busy working with the new gear-box so that the last two vehicles could set off as soon as possible for Novo. He looked up, spanner in hand. "Tell everyone there's a delay. I've just organised a quick tour of the U.S. base for the pilot so he can warm up." Then he smiled. "By the way, I had a meeting there last night. They've had time to look at the Peace Messages. Decided they quite like the idea after all. In fact, they're delighted. They're going to find somewhere special to display them."

I wanted to hug him – but he was all greasy, and a military

commander.

So, the energy had changed at the base. The warm heart of the Messages had already started their work. The shift was underway.

As I turned and plodded across ever-moving whale snow-drifts, an alarm went off. It was my explorer watch telling me it was sched-call time to phone in that I was still alive. I decided to leave it as a daily alarm. It wasn't a bad sort of a reminder. I noticed then the Tibetan band that I always wore on my wrist had gone. Well, anywhere here was a suitable place for it to lie.

We sorted rubbish and human waste to be returned with the vehicles to Novo, pulled down the tent and packed it away. In spite of our misgivings it had worked brilliantly, as had all the gear. I looked over at the Pole area. "Goodbye South Pole," I whispered. "Thank you." In the true spirit of impermanence it had already moved on. During the six days we'd been here, the ice-sheet had shifted 20 centimetres towards the Weddell Sea.

We loaded our pulks onto the plane and waited with the others. Even out of the wind it seemed to be as cold as anything we'd experienced. My hands and feet had both gone numb. I jumped up and down to try and get some circulation going. The news was that it was hot in Novo. Only minus 10°C!

Eventually, the pilot and his assistant arrived. The engines were fired up and the doors shut, but there appeared to be a problem. Even with much revving and jolting we couldn't move. We were frozen to the spot. The pilot got off with a sledge hammer and a block of wood. We heard bashing and banging noises. We learned that the landing of these old adapted planes causes the skids to create friction heat which melts ice, then refreezes. The pilots usually taxi and stop a couple of times when landing in order to clear it. The extreme cold here had prevented this from happening.

At length we were able to go. We taxied slowly past the different shaped buildings and equipment of the base. We turned around, the engines roared and we raced down the ice runway, bumping and swaying. The wings wavered and took the strain. The plane left the ground. My hand clasped involuntarily over the citrine crystal in my pocket as heaviness turned to lightness, the vibration changed and quite unexpectedly, it pulled me up too. Effortlessly, timelessly I was flying:

On either side of me there are shining beings of light with huge wings. I see the Earth beneath us glowing with rose quartz pink surrounded by golden light. We are the golden light as we fly. I am guided around the Earth, shown scenes as we pass by, touching snap-shots of time and space. The Kremlin in Moscow, a Manhattan street, icy wastes of Inuit land, heads bent in prayer in London, the peaks of the Alps, on and on, yak herders in Tibet, animals running on the plains of Africa, wet jungles of the Amazon, a mighty river in China, the dry outback of Australia... on and on... around in a golden spiral, we engulf the Earth in golden light, on and on... as shining beings of light we fly together. All is perfect. All is well.

Something brought me back with a jolt. I could feel my day-sack pressing against my legs, the prayer flags on it now battered and torn. Gaius was squashed up against my arm. Shakily, I scraped the ice from the window with a gloved finger and stared out at the receding buildings, then down at the ocean of whiteness. I gasped, and looked at my explorer watch. For a moment, I held my breath as though this would make time stand still.

Then I turned to Pete. "Wow! How awesome!" I said softly, shaking my head. "You know what? We've just gone over our special spot where we placed the crystals, and you'll never believe this, it was at exactly 9pm."

He leaned over and kissed me.

"Hey there," called the Warrior, with a wink from the other side of the plane. "I've got a gift for you." He held out a little roll of new Tibetan prayer flags. "I acquired them in the Himalayas and was going to put them at the South Pole, but it seemed more fitting for you to have them. Make sure you fly them somewhere special."

"Yes, thank you. We will." There was still one more zone of the Earth to cover...

Peace Messages

I hope we all could try to take better care of the environment so the Earth can take care of us for many years to come. (Stian) • Live out your dreams; don't dream your life away. (Rune) • One planet; respect it! (Ben) • May we all continue to explore and have adventures in new places; and have the strength to improve women's health worldwide. (Ed) • Waste not. (James) • Take a minute; be here and now. (Christian) • For us to live sustainably in our environment. (Gary) • People to stop fighting because of religion. (Gaz) • You are amazing. Keep up the good work you awesome hippies. Here's to ten thousand schools and ten million happy children. (Rachel) • Listen to the silence. (Phil) • Respect all living things and the Earth for the benefit of all future generations. (Hylton) • I hope that everyone in the world finds a great team to help them live their dreams! (Mark) • There's no point worrying about the things you can't change, because you can't change them. Nor the things that you can change, because you can change them. (Simon) • Peace; Harmony and Respect; this is our home, our Earth; let us treat our lifeline with the love she deserves. (Alexis) • Tolerance and respect. (Keith) • Appreciate the luxury you are living in. (Georg) • I set the intention to be a shining human. • Go out into the sunshine and be happy. • It is an unfailing law that the Light never abandons its soldiers. • Let go of fear and welcome instead trust and love into all our lives. • Come to the cliff, he said. They said, we are afraid. Come to the cliff, he said. They came. He pushed them and they flew. • Ice and snow virginal in its presence, showing you a new path. Nature weaving a thread of light around you. May the Divine light bless this journey, bringing you fulfilment in the task at hand. • Deep Peace of the Running Wave to you. Deep Peace of the Flowing Air to you. Deep Peace of the Quiet Earth to you. Deep Peace of the Shining Stars to you. • May Peace **truly** take root within my being and yours. • May transcendent light and love engulf the world and ease all suffering. • I will clean up my messes. • I wish not to forget that daily challenges make life's rich tapestry more beautiful. • Planet Earth keep spinning. • Think happy thoughts and you can fly. • Life is a miracle. • May all mankind live together as brothers and sisters. May Tibet regain freedom one day. • In every respect may I share your shadows upon the snow.

Within the vast Antarctic wilderness lies the future of our salvation.
• May Peace reign for all time. May we find it in our hearts and in
the heart of the world. • When you are down to nothing, God's up to
something. • Buddha said, 'All that we are is the result of what we have
thought'. I will try to be mindful. • Let your gentleness be evident to
all. The Lord is near. Don't be anxious about anything, but ineverything
by prayer and petition with thanksgiving present your requests to God,
which transcends all. Understanding will guard your hearts and minds
in Christ Jesus. • May the children of Tibet retain the gentle character
of all Tibetans and may they one day know lasting peace and happiness
in a free Tibet. • I promise to share and not be greedy. • May the love
light and peace of the one great heart go out to all hearts on Earth. •
Faith, Hope and Love, but the greatest is Love. • The ego is the barrier
to awakening. • Please let all beings live in peace and harmony, let
us help the sick, poor and aged of all nations, let us work together
compassionately to make our dreams come true. • I pledge to listen
more in my relationships to help bring harmony. • When the voice is
quiet, when we think before we speak, when we love those we know
as much as those we have yet to meet… then we will have peace. •
The most intelligent forms of life know they live due to the support of
other forms of life. To all the creators, supporters and soothers of life,
thank you. I support you. • We must not forget, that only we together
can bring peace to this planet. • No Anger, No Greed, No Envy, No
Need, Just One World In Peace And Love Is The Seed. • May peace and
harmony be the power influencing every particle of life on this beautiful
planet. • I choose to build and share my inner peace… love abound.
• May there be clear skies. • 'Human survival depends on living in
harmony and on always choosing the path of non-violence in resolving
our differences.' Dalai Lama. Let us take heed. • Sharing the best in
myself. • I pray that all of humanity may learn to live in peace and
harmony and that there could be an end to suffering. • May everyone
find peace within themselves. • I will respect all beings. • May all
beings on earth live in harmony together forever in the future and
beyond. • There are thirty million species on this Earth. They are my
family. • May the consciousness of all mankind be raised to recognize
the oneness of all life. • Let love and light fill every human heart. • May
the wisdom and compassion of the Buddha inspire the world leaders
to seek peace. • May the whole world unite in Love. • I wish for my
children to see all the beauty of the Earth. • May light spread to the
four corners of the planet bringing peace and harmony. • Let there be
peace on Earth. • There's so much of everything, it's easy to miss the
nothing. • Joy Love Peace in the spirit of The One. • May we all show
Love and Compassion to our Animal Brethren. • Thank you for my
friends, God. • I chose to share. • Protect the planet for the future of
our children. May we learn from our mistakes and move forward to
peace, food for all and a safe home for everyone. • A fountain of light
love and truth pours and sprinkles over the Earth. • May the light of

the Star shine in every human heart. • Let all the peoples of the Earth pray together. • Please help us to have peace within. • Prayer for love, compassion, respect, harmony and balance throughout the Earth. • I pray that all the world will live in peace and no one will have to fight or be hungry. • Thank you God for the birds. We'll try and take care of them and not hurt them. • May everyone have access to clean drinking water. • May the rays of compassion shine across the Earth. • I pledge that I will try every day to contribute positively to the harmony and peace of our Mother Earth • Go as a pilgrim and seek out danger. Far from comfort and well-lit avenues of life. Pit your very soul against the unknown. And seek stimulation in the company of the brave. Experience cold and hunger, heat and thirst. And survive to see another challenge and another dawn. Only then will you be at peace with yourself. And able to know and to say: "I looked down at the farthest side of the mountain. And, fulfilled and understanding all, I am truly content that I lived a full life and that was of my own choice." • And all things, whatsoever ye shall ask in prayer, believing, ye shall receive. • Sir Ernest Shackleton, didn't make it all the way South, but he did not give up and showed the world a new resoluteness. May your outer journey become an inner one and the quality of love you attract always grow as you go into the whiteness, into the brightness and, God willing, all the way there. • A wish to free all beings to eternal peace and no more suffering. May I become a Buddha for the benefit of all sentient beings. • I love you my dear Earth. • Aim for the moon and if you don't succeed you will be amongst the stars. • See the good in everyone. We all have a story to tell. • Om Mani Padme Hum. • Peace in the world depends on peace in the hearts of individuals. • I will stroke my cat. • I promise to work on my own greed thereby diminishing the greed of the Earth. • I will help my Grandma to get better. • Fly the flag for peace in men's hearts and minds, peace from the top to the bottom of the Earth. • Today has 86,400 seconds. I will use one to say 'thank you'. • I pray that survival of the fittest will pass. Whilst one child starves in Africa, humanity starves. • Care for our environment. • Look after polar bears. • Grannies make the world go round. • May the long time sun shine upon you, all love surround you and the pure light within guide your way on. • I pledge to question how the action I take will affect the poorest person I can think of. • Life is too precious to rush. • May every day be filled with smiles ...

Acknowledgements

Warm and heartfelt thanks to all family and friends who have wonderfully supported and encouraged us through the training, the race and the writing of the book. This helped us find the extraordinary amounts of dedication and endurance needed.

With special thanks to:

His Holiness the Dalia Lama for his inspiration and Universal Love. The other patrons – Joanna Lumley, Uri Geller, Doug Scott and Princess Helena Moutafian for their belief in the spirit of Climb For Tibet and its work for peace.

All those who have so freely given Peace Messages, sponsorship and heart energy.

Lawley, my three sons, Paul, Scottie and Marco and their partners, Claudia, Nella and Chloe for unending support and immeasurable love which makes all things possible.

All whose names walk across these pages in the unfolding of the story, especially my soul partner Pete for allowing the sharing of our innermost struggles in the darkest moments and for always being there for me with love and patience.

Ivy Smith and Master Advarr for guidance at a wider level and the world expansion of light.

Martha for wonderful editing and Dan, Tobias, Helen, Emily, Sally, Elaine, Dennis and all at Eye Books and Can of Worms for their care and vision.

Tony and the South Pole Race team for enabling the race to happen.

Also the crystal holders; all at White Eagle Lodge; Andy Vinsen website; Andy Webb circuit training; Mannatech nutritional and sport supplements; Yin Yang skin care; Ollie Films; Natural Balance Foods; Mid-Suffolk Leisure Centre; Papworth Hospital; Caduceus magazine; BeechTree Consultancy; AccuVision; Holistic Channel; Mary; Beverley; Gautam; Matty; Rima; George; Pawo; Dorje; Kitesh and Mir.

Those in spirit who held my hand.

Gina for sending the Emperor Gaius to keep us warm on the inside.

eyeSight

Our greatest fear is not that we are inadequate, our greatest fear is that we are powerful beyond measure. By shining your light, you subconsciously give permission to others to shine theirs.
Nelson Mandela

Travel can be a liberating experience, as it was for me in 1990, when I was just one hundred yards from Nelson Mandela as he was released from prison. I watched this monumental occasion from on top of a traffic light, amidst a sea of enthralled onlookers.

This was the 'green light' moment that inspired the creation of Eye Books. From the chaos of that day arose an appreciation of the opportunities that the world around us offers, and the desire within me to shine a light for those whose reaction to opportunity is 'can't and don't'.

Our world has been built on dreams, but the drive is often diluted by the corporate and commercial interests offering to live those dreams for us, through celebrity culture and the increasing mechanisation and automation of our lives. Inspiration comes now from those who live outside our daily routines, from those who *challenge the way we see things*.

Eye Books was born to tell the stories of *'ordinary' people doing 'extraordinary' things*. With no experience of publishing, or the constraints that the book 'industry' imposes, Eye Books created a genre of publishing to champion those who live out their dreams.

Twelve years on, and sixty stories later, Eye Books has the same ethos. We believe that ethical publishing matters. It is not about just trying to make a quick hit, it is about publishing the stories that affect our lives and the lives of others positively. We publish the books we believe will shine a light on the lives of some and enlighten the lives of many for years to come.

Join us in the Eye Books community, and share the power these stories evoke.

Dan Hiscocks
Founder and Publisher
Eye Books

www.eye-books.com

eyeCommunity

At Eye Books we are constantly challenging the way we see things and do things. But we cannot do this alone. To that end we have created an online club, a community, where members can inspire and be inspired, share knowledge and exchange ideas. Membership is free, and you can join by visiting www. eye-books.com, where you will be able to find:

What we publish
Books that truly inspire, by people who have given their all, triumphed over adversity, lived their lives to the full. Visit the dedicated microsites we have for each of our books online.

Why we publish
To champion those 'ordinary' people doing extraordinary things. The real celebrities of our world who tell stories that celebrate life to the full, not just for 15 minutes. Books where fact is more compelling than fiction.

How we publish
Eye Books is committed to ethical publishing. Many of our books feature and campaign for various good causes and charities. We try to minimise our carbon footprint in the manufacturing and distribution of our books.

Who we publish
Many, indeed most of our authors have never written a book before. Many start as readers and club members. If you feel strongly that you have a book in you, and it is a book that is experience driven, inspirational and life affirming, visit the 'How to Become an Author' page on our website. We are always open to new authors.

Eye-Books.com Club is an ever-evolving community, as it should be, and benefits from all that our members contribute, with invitations to book launches, signings and author talks, plus special offers and discounts on the books we publish.

Eye Books membership is free, and it's easy to sign up. Visit our website. Registration takes less than a minute.

www.eye-books.com

eyeBookshelf — www.eye-books.com

THE AMERICAS / ASIA

Category	Thunder & Sunshine — *Alastair Humphreys*	The Good Life — *Dorian Amos*	The Good Life Gets Better — *Dorian Amos*	Cry From the Highest Mountain — *Tess Burrows*	Riding the Outlaw Trail — *Simon Casson & Richard Adamson*	Trail of Visions Route 2 — *Vicki Couchman*	Riding with Ghosts — *Gwen Maka*	Riding with Ghosts – South of the Border — *Gwen Maka*	Lost Lands Forgotten Stories — *Alexandra Pratt*	Frigid Women — *Sue & Victoria Riches*	Touching Tibet — *Niema Ash*	First Contact — *Mark Anstice*	Tea for Two — *Polly Benge*	Baghdad Business School — *Heyrick Bond Gunning*
eyeThinker		●		●		●	●	●	●	●		●	●	●
eyeAdventurer	●	●			●		●	●	●	●	●		●	●
eyeQuirky								●						
eyeCyclist	●						●	●					●	
eyeRambler														
eyeGift	●							●						
eyeSpiritual														

THE AMERICAS | **ASIA**

AFRICA / EUROPE

Category	Moods of Future Joys — *Alastair Humphreys*	Green Oranges on Lion Mountain — *Emily Joy*	Zohra's Ladder — *Pamela Windo*	Walking Away — *Charlotte Metcalf*	Changing the World from the inside out — *Michael Meegan*	All Will Be Well — *Michael Meegan*	Seeking Sanctuary — *Hilda Reily*	Crap Cycle Lanes — *Captain Crunchynutz*	50 Quirky Bike Rides…in England and Wales — *Rob Ainsley*	On the Wall with Hadrian — *Bob Bibby*	Special Offa — *Bob Bibby*	The European Job — *Jonathan Booth*	Fateful Beauty — *Natalie Hodgson*	Slow Winter — *Alex Hickman*
eyeThinker		●	●	●	●	●	●							●
eyeAdventurer	●					●					●		●	●
eyeQuirky							●	●						
eyeCyclist	●						●	●						
eyeRambler								●	●					
eyeGift	●							●	●					
eyeSpiritual					●	●								

AFRICA | **EUROPE**

www.eye-books.com

www.eye-books.com eye**Bookshelf**

ASIA / AUS

Categories: eyeThinker · eyeAdventurer · eyeQuirky · eyeCyclist · eyeRambler · eyeGift · eyeSpiritual

- Travels in Outback Australia — *Andrew Stevenson* (AUS)
- Last of the Nomads — *W J Peasley*
- Prickly Pears of Palestine — *Hilda Reilly*
- Jasmine and Arnica — *Nicola Naylor*
- Good Morning Afghanistan — *Waseem Mahmood*
- Behind the Veil — *Lydia Laube*
- Siberian Dreams — *Andy Home*
- The Jungle Beat — *Roy Follows*
- My Journey with a Remarkable Tree — *Ken Finn*
- Fever Tress of Borneo — *Mark Eveleigh*
- Desert Governess — *Phyllis Ellis*
- Trail of Visions — *Vicki Couchman*
- Jungle Janes — *Peter Burden*

EUROPE / CROSS CONTINENT

Categories: eyeThinker · eyeAdventurer · eyeQuirky · eyeCyclist · eyeRambler · eyeGift · eyeSpiritual

- More Traveller's Tales from Heaven and Hell — *Various*
- Further Traveller's Tales from Heaven and Hell — *Various*
- Traveller's Tales from Heaven and Hell — *Various*
- Blood Sweat and Charity — *Nick Stanhope*
- Triumph Around the World — *Robbie Marshall*
- Discovery Road — *Tim Garratt & Andy Brown*
- Great Sects — *Adam Hume Kelly*
- Death — *Herbie Brennan*
- Around the World with 1000 Birds — *Russell Boyman*
- Travels with my Daughter — *Niema Ash*
- Forensics Handbook — *Pete Moore*
- Con Artist Handbook — *Joel Levy*
- The Accidental Optimist's Guide to Life — *Emily Joy*

www.eye-books.com

eyeClassics

Riding with Ghosts, Gwen Maka
£7.99

Gwen Maka's love affair with America and low budget travel began when she stepped off a plane at JFK airport in 1982 with £100 in her pocket, on her way to study underdevelopment on a Sioux reservation. This is the inspiring story of her solo cycle from Seattle to Mexico, tracing the history of Native Americans.

Frigid Women, Sue and Victoria Riches
£7.99

'Women wanted to walk to North Pole' the advertisement read. Mother and daughter, Sue & Victoria Riches never imagined how much one small article in a newspaper would change their lives..... Within two years, they were trekking across the frozen wilderness that is the Arctic Ocean, as part of the first all women's expedition to the North Pole. At times totally terrifying and at times indescribably beautiful, it was a trip of a lifetime. Having survived cancer treatment and a mastectomy it was an opportunity to discover that ANYTHING is possible if you put your mind to it, and if you WANT to succeed.

www.eye-books.com

Jasmine and Arnica, Nicola Naylor
£7.99

When Nicola lost her sight, her world collapsed. Institutionalised and misunderstood, she spent the next seven years coming to terms with an issue she had spent her life denying. Eventually she started to piece together her shattered life through a new found interest in massage. She decided to travel India alone, researching Indian massage techniques and holistic therapy. Jasmine and Arnica is the powerful and sensorial story of this seminal trip.

Green Oranges on Lion Mountain, Emily Joy
£7.99

When your dad can crash his aeroplane into two water buffalo, life is unlikely to go according to plan. Even so, Emily Joy puts on her rose-tinted specs, leaves behind her comfortable life as a Western doctor and head off for two years to volunteer in a remote hospital in West Africa. This is the true account of her posting in Sierra Leone; adventure and romance were on the agenda, rebel forces and civil war were not.

www.eye-books.com

eyeBookshelf

Touching Tibet, Niema Ash
£9.99

Niema Ash was one of the first people to enter Tibet when its borders were briefly opened to Westerners in 1986. In this highly absorbing and personal account, she relates with wit, compassion and sensitivity her encounters with people whose humour, spirituality and sheer enthusiasm for life have carried them through years of oppression and suffering. A truly touching tale.

Changing the World, Michael Meegan
£9.99

Many people say they want to make a difference in the world, but they don't know how. Changing the world offers examples of how real people have made real differences on all levels, global, local and personal. It reminds us to see the joy and love in every moment of every day. And that making a difference is something everyone can do.

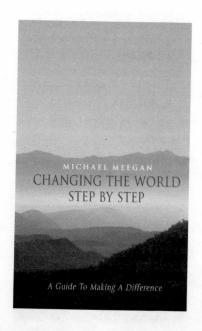

www.eye-books.com

"I am pleased to offer my prayers to
Climb for Tibet and all that it touches."

His Holiness the Dalai Lama

Climb for Tibet Tune-in

We invite you to take part in our tune-in to help the peace and harmony of
the Earth. This is a peace focus which takes place for six minutes at 6:00pm
(British Time) on the sixth day of every month. People around the world simply
hold thoughts for peace. It does not matter where you physically are, but a
quiet mind concentrating for a few minutes contributes in a powerful way. It
helps to think of the symbol of the six-pointed star sending out rays of light and
peace to all beings.

Do join us. With love and respect,

Tess and Pete

Visit **www.climbfortibet.org** to send us a Peace Message for our next event,
or to read the complete Master Advarr guidance. You can also contact us by
emailing **tessburrows@yahoo.co.uk**.

To read more about Tess or to order more copies of this book and/or *Cry from
the Highest Mountain* visit: **www.canofwormsenterprises.co.uk/authors**

eyeAuthor

Tess Burrows

Tess Burrows was born in Southern England in 1948 and educated at Bedales School. She gained a degree in Ecological Science from Edinburgh University and moved to Australia to grow trees. In 1984 she returned as the mother of three young boys, with the gentleness of motherhood being paramount. In 1990, hit by the realisation that it is possible to help the Earth and make a difference, she started climbing and using this medium for a number of unusual events raising awareness and funds for charity.

In 1998 she founded Climb For Tibet with her partner Pete. Together they undertook various "peace climbs", raising over £100,000 for building schools in Tibet for underprivileged children.

Best-selling author of *Cry from The Highest Mountain*, climbing instructor, healer, motivational speaker and grandmother of two little girls – one of whom was born the same day as this book.

She is a believer in the joy and positivity of life.

Also by Tess Burrows:
Cry from the Highest Mountain
£9.99
"An enthralling journey of courage and endurrance."
Joanna Lumley

Their goal was to climb to the point furthest from the centre of the Earth, some 2,150 metres higher than the summit of Everest. The mission: to promote Earth Peace. For Tess it became a struggle of body and mind, as she was driven towards the highest point within herself.

Altitude sickness, blizzards and lack of experience were just a few of the problems that stood between the team and their goal: the summit. Would courage and belief carry them through, against the odds?

www.eye-books.com